Swedenborg
AND New Paradigm Science

Swedenborg Studies / No. 10
Monographs of the Swedenborg Foundation

Swedenborg
AND New Paradigm Science

Ursula Groll

Translated by
Nicholas Goodrick-Clarke

Foreword by
David Lorimer

Swedenborg Foundation Publishers
West Chester, Pennsylvania

Originally published in German as Ursula Groll, *Emanuel Swedenborg und das Neue Zeitalter* (St. Goar, Germany: Reichl Verlag, 1993).

Swedenborg Studies is a scholarly series published by the Swedenborg Foundation. The primary purpose of the series is to make materials available for understanding the life and thought of Emanuel Swedenborg (1688–1772) and the impact his thought has had on others. The Foundation undertakes to publish original studies and English translations of such studies and to republish primary sources that are otherwise difficult to access. Proposals should be sent to: Senior Editor, Swedenborg Studies, Swedenborg Foundation, 320 North Church Street, West Chester, Pennsylvania 19380.

Library of Congress Cataloging-in-Publication Data

Groll, Ursula
    [Emanuel Swedenborg und das Neue Zeitalter. English]
    Swedenborg and new paradigm science / Ursula Groll ; translated by Nicholas Goodrick-Clarke ; foreword by David Lorimer
       p. cm. -- (Swedenborg studies ; no. 10)
    Includes bibliographical references (p.) and index.
    ISBN 0-87785-303-7 (pb)
    1. Swedenborg, Emanuel, 1688-1772. I. Title. II. Series.

BX8711 .G7613 2000
289.4'092--dc21

                          00-041989

Designed by Christian Ledgerwood, Orcas, Washington
Set in Sabon by Christian Ledgerwood
Printed in the United States of America.

CONTENTS

FOREWORD

My first encounter with Emanuel Swedenborg came via a footnote to the famous poem *Correspondances* by Charles Baudelaire. I had read elsewhere of Swedenborg's influence on other writers such as Blake and Balzac, but I was sufficiently intrigued by the footnote to borrow a biography of Swedenborg from the university library. It lay unread on my bedside table for some weeks; then, one evening, I dipped into it and was hooked. I was immediately struck by the fact that a scientist had become a mystic without sacrificing his reason and common sense. Indeed, the same level-headed quality is apparent in both Swedenborg's scientific and mystical writings. D. T. Suzuki points out that this may be a disadvantage when extraordinary claims are made about his visionary experiences and are conveyed in the same sober prose style. However, for me, this was part of the appeal.

Since 1978, the Scientific and Medical Network and Wrekin Trust have been staging an annual Mystics and Scientists Conference in Winchester, England. The series is now in its twenty-third year. The idea was and is a bold one, providing for the presentation of both scientific and mystical thinking related to a particular theme. Swedenborg would have been a natural choice to speak at such a meeting and would be in the unusual position of being both a scientist and a mystic at the same time. Ursula Groll's book treats many of the same themes addressed at conferences over the years, and indeed the main authors investigated—Capra, Bohm, and Sheldrake—have all been speakers in the series.

Two significant themes prefigured in the book are wholeness and morphogenesis. Swedenborg's picture of heaven as a Grand Man or mesocosm conveys an organic understanding of the relationship between whole and part. Individual human beings are inseparable from the whole of humanity, itself incorporating all who have lived in the past. One of the striking quotations used in the book to illustrate this point indicates that "this all-embracing whole composed of the smallest parts is a coherent single work, that no single point touches and can be excited, without the sensation being transferred to all other parts." This sentence exactly represents modern quantum non-locality or entanglement: if associated particles are separated in space and the spin of one is altered, the spin of the other alters simultaneously, whatever the distance. Swedenborg emerges as a holist before the term was coined. With respect to formative fields and the work of Sheldrake and others, Swedenborg posits the necessity of an organizing mold or formative principle of order. As in a number of esoteric systems, this field seems to act as an intermediary between matter and spirit and is sometimes referred to as the "etheric" level. The nature of such field phenomena is still widely debated within developmental biology and requires more than a molecular explanation.

The interface between science and mysticism is a particular aspect of the more general interface between science and religion. The pioneering work in this field was initiated by William James a hundred years ago, and his *Varieties of Religious Experience* remains a classic to this day. In his day, there was a more-or-less hostile standoff between science and religion in the wake of Darwin's theory of natural selection and books by such authors as J. W. Draper and A. D. White, which emphasized the continuous tensions between the two approaches. The tension arises, in my view, from rival metaphysical claims made on behalf of religion and science. The classic scientific view has been that religion as superstition will eventually be entirely explained away by the advances of sciences. However, other more constructive forms of engagement have arisen in the last twenty years, thanks in large measure to the support given to the field by the John Templeton Foundation. No longer does one hear only about conflict, but also about complementarity and convergence of understandings.

One reason for this trend is a growing awareness among scientists themselves of inherent limitations of scientific thinking, based as it is on a set of often unacknowledged philosophical assumptions. This has become increasingly clear since the publication in the 1960s of Thomas Kuhn's *Structure of Scientific Revolutions*. These assumptions frequently contain a materialistic or physicalist bias, whereby it is assumed that only the physical world is real, that mind is the product of matter, and that brain processes give rise to consciousness. It is a bias of which Swedenborg was fully aware in his own day and about which he writes in his short work *Intercourse of the Soul and the Body.*

When he calls the hypothesis of "physical influx" or physicalism "arises from the appearance of the senses, and the fallacies then derived." The problem with this hypothesis for Swedenborg is that it is based on a threefold ignorance: "Ignorance as to what the soul is, ignorance as to what is spiritual, and ignorance respected the nature of influx—these three things must first be explained before the rational faculty can see the truth itself." And he adds, knowingly: "For hypothetical truth is not truth itself but a conjecture of the truth." He sees a danger that ignorance of the existence of a spiritual world could make a person "so far infatuated as to become an atheistic materialist," remarking that his mission was precisely to enlighten people about the nature of spiritual worlds in a manner acceptable to the critical intellect. Those who know nothing of these worlds, he says, are liable to fall into blindness, "because the minds, depending solely on the sight of the eye, becomes in its reasonings like a bat, which flies by night in a wandering course"; into darkness because the sight of the eye is deprived of all spiritual light; and into stupidity, "because the man still thinks, but from natural things concerning spiritual, and not contrariwise."

This pattern has characterized much mainstream scientific thinking since Swedenborg's time and down to our own. It can be traced back to Descartes and Galileo with their sharp distinction between primary and secondary qualities: the former are quantifiable, measurable, tangible, extended in time and space, while the latter are qualitative and intangible, constituting features now attributed to consciousness. The following table summarizes the direction of such thinking.

Causality and Explanation

Primary	*Secondary*
External/visible	Internal/invisible
Surface	Depth (shared)
Observation	Interpretation
Quantity	Quality
Objective	Subjective
Third person (it)	First person (I)
Matter-energy	Spirit-mind
Body/brain	Consciousness

These categories might, in turn, be expressed as:

Experiment	Experience
Science	Spirituality

The important point to note is that the right-hand column is explained in terms of the left, defined as primary. Science has tended to take an outside-in view or third-person perspective, while mystics inhabit a world seen from the inside out, where first-person perspectives and subjective experience are primary. It can also be seen that this causal direction of thinking necessarily involves the hypothesis that brain and body give rise to consciousness and mind. The corollary of this assumption is that consciousness ceases to exist at bodily death, a state entirely contradictory to Swedenborg's own experiences and consequent theory.

Swedenborg describes his own view of the relationship between body and soul as "spiritual influx," arguing that "the soul is a spiritual substance, and therefore purer, prior and interior, but the body is material, and therefore grosser, posterior and exterior, and it is according to order that the purer should flow into the grosser, the prior into the posterior, and the interior into the exterior, thus what is spiritual into what is material and not vice versa." The reader can appreciate that Swedenborg's position is the complete reverse of the materialistic understanding that the brain gives rise to consciousness. His experiences also convinced him absolutely of the existence of life after death in a spiritual realm—it was no hypothetical conjecture for him, but rather a fact of everyday life:

> I am well aware that many will say that no one can possibly speak with spirits and angels so long as he lives in the body; and many will say that it is all fancy, others that I relate such things in order to gain credence. . . . But by all this I am not deterred, for I have seen, I have heard, I have felt. (*Arcana Coelestia* 68)

My first researches in the 1970s, after reading Swedenborg, were a quest for parallels with his writings in the twentieth century. I found some resonance in early spiritualist classics such as W. Stainton Moses, then a much more systematic and profound treatment in the work of Rudolf Steiner. I also read the major scientific and philosophical works on the survival question. Some minor sources added pieces to the jigsaw and built up a coherent picture that differs scarcely at all from Swedenborg's own common-sense descriptions. He defines here the nature of the soul and its relation to the body:

> As regards the soul, of which it is said that it will live after death, it is nothing else than the man himself who lives within the body, that is, the interior man who in this world acts through the body, and who causes the body to live. This man, when loosed from the body, is called a spirit. (*Arcana Coelestia* 6054)

Death is, therefore, the separation of the spirit from the body. This phenomenology is repeated time and again both in reports of near-death experiences (NDEs) and in cases where subjects are hypnotically regressed to the experience of death in a previous incarnation (more on reincarnation below). The expression used most frequently is that of "floating out of the body." As Swedenborg puts it: "Yet the man does not die; he is merely separated from the corporeal part that was of use to him in the world, for the man himself lives" (that is, is conscious). Swedenborg himself describes an experience of death designed to give him a first-hand understanding.

One serious problem observed by Swedenborg and other adepts and sensitives since his time is that many people do not realize that they have died: "I may state that much experience has shown me that when a man comes into the other life he is not aware that he is in that life, but supposes that he is still in the world, and even that he is still in the body." This arises from a complete lack of any conception of another realm of existence, so much so that, when people find themselves still conscious, they cannot but think that they must still be physically alive. They draw a false conclusion from an incorrect premise, namely:

Physical life is the only form of conscious existence.
I am still conscious.
Therefore, I am still in physical existence.

This interpretation wears a little thin when people find themselves unable to communicate with their loved ones (who treat them as if they were not there!) and even seem to pass through physical matter altogether. When the significance of these anomalies becomes clear to them, they are ready to understand that they have moved on. If such events are commonplace, they highlight the need for education so that people have at least a "rough guide" to what to expect in the next stage of their inner journey.

I return now to William James, a thinker who was influenced by Swedenborg, initially through his father's interest. James was unusual in being not only a psychologist, but a philosopher and psychical researcher as well. His researches spanned these disciplines, giving his thinking a breadth that psychology was to lose with the rise of behaviorism and the influence of the German school of experimental psychology. It is significant that in 1911, the year after James's death, Harvard refused an endowment to establish a chair of psychical research, fearing for its reputation. Many of the same arguments were being advanced in the early 1980s when a number of distinguished universities made sure that the Koestler Chair of Parapsychology went elsewhere. Only with the rise of consciousness studies in the 1990s are some areas of psychology recovering the kind of breadth of visions that characterized the writings of William James.

In addition to its Mystics and Scientists Conference, The Scientific and Medical Network has held three meetings on the theme "Beyond the Brain," at which James and indeed Swedenborg would have been keynote presenters in their day. The conference is unusual even today in its openness to the possibility that the mind may not be entirely dependent on brain processes. The theme for 1999 asked the question if consciousness seemed to extend beyond birth and death. It is a question that Swedenborg would have answered in the affirmative regarding death but not with respect to birth as he made it quite clear, as Groll points out, that he did not subscribe to the doctrine of reincarnation.

It is perhaps surprising that a poll found that twenty-four percent of Catholics believe the heretical doctrine of reincarnation. Swedenborg's rejection of this view is entirely orthodox, despite some recent apologists' attempts to claim that Jesus really did teach it. It is foreign to Hebrew doctrine and comes into Western thought from Plato, who, in turn, may have inherited it from India via Egypt. The most rigorous modern scientific research in this field has been carried out by Professor Ian Stevenson, who has investigated the claimed memories of over two thousand children since the 1960s. Stevenson is scrupulous in weighing up the evidence and inferring possible theoretical interpretations from it. He considers Swedenborg's theory—that the children are possessed by the memories of a surviving spirit—most carefully. It is hard to rule this interpretation out altogether since there is little doubt that the memories indeed belong to a deceased person. The question, though, is the nature of the relationship between the child and those memories: is another individual remembering through that child's brain or is there some more intimate link via the soul? Readers need to make up their own minds, but only when they have carefully weighed Stevenson's findings.

A final theme that I would like to consider is the relationship between science and spirituality. For people like Swedenborg, there is no contradiction involved. The universe is one and needs to be understood as a whole. Unlike many scientists, he was emphatically not wedded to a materialist understanding. However, most scientists begin by trying to understand the world from the outside in and apply this approach to the study of consciousness by measuring the quantifiable aspects of brain function. Only later may they consider their own consciousness as part of the question and begin to acquire a modicum of self-knowledge. As soon as this process gets under way, the scientist or knower becomes a first-person participator rather than a third-person observer: his or her consciousness is directly affected and involved. Then the transformation of the knower becomes a real possibility. This is the promise of consciousness studies: that scientists will find their understanding of reality transformed as they go deeper into it and that science as a whole will change as a result. It will not lose its rigor, but will become more open to subtle aspects of reality and indeed to compassion or love and wisdom, as Swedenborg would have put it.

By linking the pioneering work of Swedenborg with some of the most creative scientific thinking of our own day, Ursula Groll has opened up new avenues of understanding on Swedenborg, while simultaneously throwing light on eighteenth-century anticipations of modern holistic ideas. This book will provide Swedenborgians with a wider angle on Swedenborg, while introducing Swedenborg's work to a new public interested in holistic science and spirituality.

David Lorimer
President, Swedenborg Society (London)
Director, Scientific and Medical Network

ABOUT THE TRANSLATION

Ursula Groll's *Emanuel Swedenborg und das Neue Zeitalter* was originally published in 1993 by Reichl Verlag. In order to make the present translation more accessible to readers of English, some changes have been made.

(1) Quotations from the writings of Emanuel Swedenborg, which Ursula Groll extracted from German translations of Swedenborg's works, are taken from English versions currently in publication, particularly from the redesigned Standard Edition of the Works of Emanuel Swedenborg, 30 volumes, issued by the Swedenborg Foundation from 1993 through 1998 (see "Bibliography of Works by Emanuel Swedenborg").

(2) Ursula Groll also occasionally referenced material from German translations of books originally published in English. For the reader's convenience, wherever possible the English editions are cited, with the corresponding page numbers.

INTRODUCTION

The visionary work of Emanuel Swedenborg is all of a piece, a self-contained whole. His assertions must be set in a universal context, but this is not immediately accessible to the reader of a single book. The following study presents an outline of the Swedenborgian worldview. It seeks to make transparent the complexity of his whole opus. As Swedenborg's visionary writings are not systematically divided into various topics, we shall examine the subject under six headings.

First, a biographical survey of Swedenborg's life and his path towards the perception of absolute truth. The theme is his transformation from a natural scientist to a visionary.

The chapter "The All-Embracing Whole" demonstrates, by comparing Swedenborg's statements and the findings of modern science, especially quantum physics, how this totality—the universe—coheres and maintains itself.

The chapter "Consciousness" shows how the all-embracing spirit forms material and penetrates the whole universe. In particular, the findings of Rupert Sheldrake, a biochemist in search of the development of forms in nature, are compared with Swedenborg's statements concerning the development of forms in the whole universe, in both the spiritual and material realms. Against this vast backdrop, we find that humankind is a collaborator in creation through each person's individual consciousness. In this way, each person makes his or her own contribution, according to the individual's spiritual level, towards the future and the evolution of humankind.

"Spiritual Rebirth" is the central theme in the visionary work of Swedenborg. As the crown of creation, and as the microcosm in the macrocosm, humanity is created in the image of God. Through the development of the divine light and the inner centers of consciousness, which correspond to the seven days of creation in Genesis according to Swedenborg, this transformation occurs through conversion (*metanoia*) from the outer to the inner human being. People can thereby regain the original unity with God that was lost through the Fall and recognize the true ground of Being, which is hidden behind and within the world of material phenomena.

"The New Age" or "The New Paradigm" is not identical in Swedenborg's parlance with its current usage. Swedenborg calls it the "New Church." This New Church is no institution, but composed of those persons who have transformed themselves from within, in whom the divine light unfolds through conversion, and who are thus on their way back to the original unity. This is Swedenborg's signpost to a future for all mankind.

That side of existence inaccessible to the natural senses is illuminated in the chapter "Life after Death." According to Swedenborg, the step of conscious evolution and the harmonization of the inner and the outer being only become evident in the next world. Spiritual development in this world is a preparation for the true spiritual life of the next. This preparation continues into eternity in the next world, on the corresponding level of consciousness, which the individual achieved during his or her earthly life. There, the circle closes and the self-contained wholeness is made manifest—in this world and the next—an ever-present reality in Swedenborg's work.

The Swedenborg quotations in this book have been chosen so as to reflect the Swedenborgian worldview as representatively as possible. As Swedenborg's texts flow into one another, it is often helpful to give relatively long and continuous quotations, rather than interrupt the line of thought through commentary. This also makes it possible to familiarize the reader with Swedenborg's own texts and literary style. Quotations are drawn exclusively from the English translations published by the Swedenborg Foundation in West Chester. Both the literary works of Swedenborg and the secondary literature cannot be easily surveyed on account of their enormous volume. Most publications on Swedenborg have been published in English. They are so numerous that they can scarcely all be listed. But William Ross Woofenden's *Swedenborg Researcher's Manual* (Bryn Athyn, Penna.: Swedenborg Scientific Association, 1988) provides a good and helpful survey of all Swedenborg's publications, as well as a large selection of secondary literature in various languages.

Ursula Groll

Chapter 1

Life, Work, and Influence

When Emanuel Swedenborg began to write his extensive visionary works in the middle of the eighteenth century, he had already published a comparable number of scientific works embracing all fields of contemporary research. Swedenborg's graduation from natural scientist to visionary seemed predestined.

Emanuel Swedenborg was born the son of the court preacher, Jesper Swedberg, on January 29, 1688, in Stockholm. His date of birth refers to the old Julian calendar, which remained current in Sweden until 1740. According to the Gregorian calendar, now in general use throughout the world, Swedenborg's birthday would fall on February 9.

In 1719, the Swedberg family was raised to the nobility and henceforth bore the name Swedenborg. In 1702, his father was nominated Bishop of Skara and moved to Brunsbo, a small place in central Sweden, and left the young Emanuel in the care of his brother-in-law, Erik Benzelius the Younger (1675–1743), in the conservative and venerable university town of Uppsala. Benzelius was the librarian of the University of Uppsala and later Professor of Theology, before he became Bishop of Linkøping. He introduced

Emanuel to the world of Swedish humanism, the citadel of which was the University of Uppsala. Here Emanuel received his classical education, which embraced all arts subjects. Here he learned to write a good, classical Latin prose, in which he would later compose his visionary work. The student eventually mastered eight foreign languages fluently, including Greek, Hebrew, Latin, English, French, German, Italian, and Dutch.

But Emanuel Swedenborg's greatest love concerned neither ancient languages nor the arts, but the natural sciences and the possibilities of their technical application. He occupied himself intensively with mathematics, geometry, astronomy, and technology. He found his great exemplar in Christopher Polhem (1661–1751), the most famous inventor and engineer of Sweden. Polhem was the prominent representative of mechanics and technology in the land and served Charles XII, King of Sweden. In due course, Swedenborg would collaborate with Polhem for many years.

But first of all, Swedenborg passionately wanted to undertake a study visit to England where the foundations of the new science were being laid. From 1710 to 1712, Swedenborg spent the initial phase of his overseas studies in the promised land of natural science. Here in England rapid developments in mathematics, astronomy, physics, mechanics, and geology were closely linked with such names as Isaac Newton (1642–1727), Edmund Halley (1656–1742), and John Flamsteed (1646–1719), along with other great scientists who had founded the famous Royal Society. Swedenborg made the acquaintance of them all.

From England, his journey led through Holland and Belgium to Paris where he had access to the Académie Royale through the recommendations of Swedish and English friends; here he made contact with great French scholars. When Swedenborg left Paris in the early summer of 1714, he tried, in vain, to visit the famous philosopher Gottfried Wilhelm Leibniz (1646–1716) in Hanover on his homeward journey to Sweden.

In 1716, Swedenborg became the assistant of Christopher Polhem; together they published the scientific journal *Daedalus*

Hyperboreus. Through the personal patronage of Charles XII, who became his close friend, Swedenborg was appointed Assessor Extraordinary of the Board of Mines, the supreme industrial authority of Sweden, a position that offered him financial security for the rest of his life. Even during his long stays abroad, the king granted him leave and the continued payment of his salary, reduced by a half in order to pay a deputy. Further research journeys to Holland, Germany, and France followed in the years from 1720 to 1722 and again from 1733 to 1734. A third journey that lasted from 1736 to 1739 led him to Rome by way of Paris, Venice, and Bologna.

By the age of 56, the unmarried Swedenborg had reached the peak of his fame as a natural scientist, especially in the areas of geometry, mathematics, metallurgy, physics, and chemistry. He was a member of the Swedish Academy of Sciences in Stockholm and the Imperial Academy of Sciences at St. Petersburg. He was a member of the Swedish Parliament up until his death. The great American philosopher, poet, and transcendentalist Ralph Waldo Emerson (1803–1882) called Swedenborg, solely on the basis of his scientific achievements, an intellectual giant whom one could scarcely grasp in a single human life. "[He] suggests, as Aristotle, Bacon, Selden, Humboldt, that a certain vastness of learning, or *quasi* omnipresence of the human soul in nature, is possible."[1] In his scientific works, Swedenborg ingeniously anticipated discoveries that were not confirmed until much later in the nineteenth and twentieth centuries. Such was the status of his researches into brain and nerve function, his atomic theory and nebular theory relating to the evolution and order of the universe, the wave theory of light, the theory of heat as motion, the theory of animal magnetism, and the explanation of electricity as a form of motion in the ether. By means of science, Swedenborg sought to lift the veil of nature and solve the riddle of life. Like Goethe's Faust, he tried to find out "what holds the world together at its innermost level" and searched for the ground of being hidden behind the manifestations of the material world. Through his anatomical studies, he hoped to find the seat of the soul in the body, whose effectiveness he tried to explain in purely mechanical principles, as had Descartes.

The extent to which he was moving away from the practical application of his research and mechanistic thinking in the course of his scientific work and moving towards his true goal, the quest of truth and understanding, can be seen from the titles of his works which are devoted almost exclusively to questions of psychology between 1733 and 1744: *Empirical Psychology* (1733); *Infinite and Final Cause of Creation* (1734); *The Mechanism of the Soul and the Body* (1734); *Knowledge of the Soul* (1739); *The Soul or Rational Psychology* (1742); and his own dream journal (1743–1744), in which he discussed his dream experiences.

Swedenborg's scientific career led him from the study of the universe and the origins of life through studies of the stars and the formation of the planets, from flying machines to mining, to an investigation of molecules, atoms, and subatomic particles. His voyage of discovery led him increasingly from the great to the small, from the outer to the inner, until he discovered the mirror of the universe, the seat of the Divine as the source of truth, in his own soul. At the very peak of his scientific fame and recognition by the European world of learning, the self-conscious and ambitious researcher discovered his true vocation. As his admirer Goethe wrote of him in the *Frankfurter Gelehrten Anzeigen* (1772), he was "the esteemed visionary of our times."

Swedenborg's transition from natural scientist to visionary was preceded by a violent inner struggle marked by great spiritual turmoil and self-doubt. For years he experienced a painful process of development, which he had described in his diaries and dream journals. In this process of inner transformation, he had surrendered his overwrought self-consciousness and burning scientific ambition. He saw that the path of empirical research, which he had traveled thus far, could solve neither the question of the origin of the universe nor the riddle of life; that science fails whenever it tries to grasp the whole world and plumb the mystery of God and the soul. At the end of his scientific researches, he left the path of empirical perception and abandoned his efforts to explain the world according to geometrical and mechanistic principles. A higher form of perception was opened up to him, surpassing scientific knowledge and abstraction and mediated true knowledge. This he called intuition.

Intuition is for Swedenborg an *a priori* perception vouchsafed to humanity alone by God. People can only open themselves completely to intuition once they have given up egoism, vanity, and arrogance. Entrusting himself to the "illumination of the divine light," Swedenborg surrenders in all humility to God's gift of grace. Intuition is for him an inner experience and stands before and above all thinking. It comes from the deepest realms of the soul, which contains all knowledge, the end of all things, and penetrates into the innermost essence of being. Scarcely anyone can intimate the knowledge gleaned by intuition better than Swedenborg: "In this way a kind of voice of reason manifests itself and gives the sign that the soul is called towards a kind of inner connection and in this very moment has fallen back into the golden age of its original condition."[2] In this blissful condition, intuition discerns the essence of things and is at one with its divine origin. The heart of Swedenborg's metaphysics lies in the ground of being, the absolute reality, knowledge of which is gained alone by intuition. This metaphysics contains both the fundamental knowledge of reality and knowledge of the world of material manifestations. This metaphysics is quite simply the science of reality or "the knowledge which enables man to distinguish between the real and the illusory and to recognize things in their essence, that is to say *in divinus*"; it is "*scientia sacra*,"[3] the knowledge of the eternal out of which the endless creation proceeds in its multiple manifestations.

During the night of April 6, 1744, the face of Jesus Christ appeared to Swedenborg in a dream. In Jesus' holiness and divinity, Swedenborg recognized the font of all being and the source of the one true knowledge. This vision of Christ was Swedenborg's fundamental religious experience. It confirmed to him that true knowledge of the absolute does not come from scientific research and analytic thought, but only through the grace of God, through the working of the divine in humankind.

Following a subsequent vision of vocation during April 1745 in London, Swedenborg felt himself chosen by God as a seer, and the future course of his life was set. God had assigned him the interpretation of the spiritual sense of the Bible for humanity. God would himself dictate what Swedenborg had to write down. The notes of his friend, the banker Carl Robsam, recount Swedenborg's oral report: "In the aforesaid night the spirit world, hell and heaven, were opened to my gaze in order to persuade me. . . from this day forward I renounced all mundane scholarship and worked only on spiritual things, according to what the Lord ordered me to write. Day after day the Lord opened the eyes of my spirit so that I was able fully wide awake to see what was happening in the other world and to converse completely waking with angels and spirits."4

Human reason and empiricism were exalted during the Enlightenment, and mechanistic thinking became almost the universal worldview. But contrary to the rationalism of his times, Swedenborg's visionary writings offered a unified world picture embracing the invisible and rationally inexplicable "beyond."

Swedenborg was very well aware that his spiritual transformation would encounter great skepticism, even antipathy and ridicule, among his contemporaries: "I know that this is incredible to many, but this is because nothing is believed which cannot be seen by the bodily eyes and felt with the hands of flesh. A person whose interiors are closed, knows nothing of the things which exist in the spiritual world or in heaven. (*Arcana Coelestia* 4622).5 Elsewhere he writes: "I know well that many will object. No one can talk with spirits and angels so long as he lives in the body: and many will say that it is all fancy, but I am not deterred, for I *have* seen, heard, and felt (*Arcana Coelestia* 68).

Something quite extraordinary had happened to Swedenborg. His burning thirst for knowledge of the ultimate things of life was slaked by "the mercy of God" that revealed to him the "face of the spirit" and allowed him to penetrate to the true essence of things: spiritual vision. In a fully conscious state, he experienced his first visions, and he described what he saw in a language that was comprehensible and appropriate to his time. He was in a heightened state of consciousness in which he had the complete control of his senses of perception. Ernst Benz expressly emphasizes that the "wakefulness of the intellect and the wakefulness of the senses" is characteristic of Swedenborg.[6] Thus, it was it possible for him to record his visions with such wonderful inner integrity and the absence of any contradiction, in the manner of his earlier scientific work.

Ever since childhood, Swedenborg had mastered a breathing technique similar to yoga exercises, which he initially applied unconsciously and later consciously whenever he was concentrating intensively on a specific problem. This technique brought about an altered state of consciousness.[7] By virtue of this "inner breath," he was able to ascend to various levels of consciousness only when he was observing, describing, or reflecting on "spiritual things," and especially whenever he had to consider a biblical passage or a very specific problem during his subsequent commentaries on the inner sense of the Bible. As Ernst Benz remarked, "meditation glides into vision."[8] Thus did the spiritual world open itself to Swedenborg.

Swedenborg repeatedly explains in his writings that he did not explicitly strive for these gifts of vision, which granted him the understanding he so deeply desired. God gave him these gifts as a servant of the truth, in order that he could communicate it to humankind. This visionary gift, pure vision, which links the soul with the ground of being and allows it to become one with the divine, is vouchsafed only to a few highly spiritually developed individuals, for example, the prophets or the great seers of Eastern religions. It is never possible in what we would call "normal," that is to say a relatively low level of consciousness. We cannot penetrate with our senses and intellect into the fundamental spiritual reality. That is what is written in the holy book of the Hindus, the *Bhagavad Gita* (ii, 29):

See, the life that fills everything
Deeply veiled in mystery.
Who can grasp it, who can fathom it,

What language can proclaim its essence?

No eye has yet glimpsed it,
No ear ever heard its voice;
Only the soul can understand,
Where sight and hearing cease.[9]

Swedenborg used his visionary gift exclusively to answer religious questions. Through the divine grace that opened his inner senses and enabled spiritual vision, he became the real enlightener in an age dominated by a rational mechanistic explanation of the universe. He saw it as his duty and mission to interpret the spiritual sense of the Bible, which he believed no mortal could understand on the basis of its literal content and sense. He felt himself called, "to give the Christian Gospel and hope new form corresponding to the modern world-view."[10] Through his exegesis of the spiritual sense of the Bible, his visionary work offers a comprehensive interpretation and representation of the universe. He shows the role and purpose of man, whose duty is to direct his entire endeavor to the cognition of the absolute.

Swedenborg's visionary gift became a matter of public knowledge following his oft-quoted description of the great fire in Stockholm on June 17, 1759, which he "saw" while a guest at a party in Gøteborg two-hundred-and-fifty miles away. His detailed report concerning the extent of the fire caused great consternation among those present. Two days later, it was confirmed in every detail. Even Immanuel Kant was so impressed that he commissioned a friend to examine the case on the spot. As we know from Kant himself, the result was positive.

Swedenborg never abused his visionary gift to get in contact with particular deceased persons, as he was all too often asked to do by friends once his capacities became widely known. He even declined the request of the Count Ludwig IX of Hesse-Darmstadt who wanted to enquire after the well-being of several mistresses and war comrades in the next world. To be sure, there were a few exceptions like Queen Louisa Ulrika of Sweden and Countess Marteville to whose requests for contact with the spirit world he acceded. But Swedenborg warned repeatedly against the great dangers of spiritualistic practice of contacting the spirit world because the spirits almost always lie. "When spirits begin to talk with a person, that individual must beware for they say almost anything, and if a person listens, they dare more and deceive and seduce him in the most varied ways" (*Spiritual Diary* 1622).

Spiritualistic practices generally lead to contact with lower levels of the spirit realm, which exercise a very negative effect on people. The normal frontiers of consciousness between humans, spirits, and angels may not be violated because they exist for good reason according to Swedenborg: "[S]ince we have separated ourselves from heaven, the Lord has provided that there should be angels and spirits with each of us and that we should be led by the Lord through them. This is the reason there is such an intimate union" (*Heaven and Hell* 247). Through this divine protection, people are preserved against evil influences and the possession of spirits because "there are also spirits called natural and physical spirits who do not unite with our thoughts when they come to us the way other spirits do but rather enter our bodies and take over all its senses, talking through our mouths and acting through our limbs. It seems to them entirely as though everything of ours were theirs. These are the spirits that obsess people; but they have been cast into hell by the Lord and moved decisively away; so obsessions like this do not occur nowadays" (*Heaven and Hell* 257).[11]

Thus, Swedenborg warns expressly against casual intimacy with the spirit world and its destructive influence on the soul of human beings, which can lead to insanity: "Take care. That way leads to the asylum. . . . I advise you never to desire such traffic or intercourse."[12] Although it is quite clear from Swedenborg's own words that he was no medium, he is often erroneously linked with "channelers" in the spiritualistic literature of recent years. In a state of trance, these human "channels" place themselves at the disposal of a supposedly higher intelligence, a being from beyond, while switching off their own will. John Klimo, the leading scholar in this field, has even called Swedenborg "the true giant of channeling literature" because he is said to have channeled for twenty-seven years—longer than any previous person.[13] Arthur Ford, himself famous as a medium, describes him as "the last great scientist of Western civilization to possess and demonstrate remarkable psychic powers."[14]

Swedenborg's renascent but dubious fame among occultists and spiritualists in recent times was largely a result of their desire to recruit a scientific genius and universal scholar as an authority to lend credibility to the spiritualistic wave. However, these spiritualists fail to make the necessary distinction between true prophetic vision and mediumism.[15]

A decade of disciplined thought and work preceded Swedenborg's visionary activity. His inner clairvoyance developed in a transformative process, which he was constantly able to consider and critically analyze in his diaries. His visions were always objective. He was wide-awake and fully conscious while receiving visions, as have been granted to very few great seers in the history of humankind. Because he was not subject to the destructive forces to which mediums are exposed—his source was of divine origin—he was able to work on his religious writings for twenty-seven years, until he was eighty-four years old, in the best of health and discipline. Only thus can his great influence in European and American intellectual history and literature right up to the present be explained. His contemporaries saw in him a wonderful benevolent and genuine person, who not only put his spiritual truths on paper, but lived according to them. The Swedish statesman Count Anders Johan von Høpken (1712–1789) wrote about Swedenborg after his death: "I have not only known him for forty-two years, but was visiting him on a daily basis. . . . He saw everything clearly and expressed himself well on every subject."[16]

Swedenborg's influence on intellectual history can only be sketched owing to its enormous range. Immanuel Kant (1724–1804), the great philosopher of the Enlightenment, stimulated the keenest interest amongst German scholars, somewhat ironically, with his notorious and destructive polemic, published anonymously in 1766. Here he describes Swedenborg's *Arcana Coelestia* as "eight quarto volumes full of nonsense" and as "the wild whims of the very worst enthusiast."[17]

But Kant damaged his own reputation more than that of Swedenborg, who was defended against Kant's defamation in many reviews of the polemic by prominent men such as Moses Mendelssohn, Johann Gottlieb Herder, Friedrich Christoph Oetinger, and Heinrich Wilhelm Clemm.[18] Due to Kant's attack, interest in Swedenborg only grew. His influence persisted so strongly in European and American thought that it inspired even the greatest figures of world literature.

The translation of Swedenborg's works into German was the life's work of the Tübingen librarian and theologian, Johann Friedrich Immanuel Tafel (1796–1863). The research of the Marburg church historian and scholar Ernst Benz (1907–1978) have contributed greatly to the recognition of Swedenborg. He demonstrated that Swedenborg was "the spiritual pioneer of German Idealism and Romanticism."[19] The influence of Swedenborg's doctrine leads from the founder of Swabian theosophy Friedrich Christoph Oetinger (1702–1782) and Johann Friedrich Oberlin (1740–1826) to the German Romantic philosophers Johann Gottlieb Herder (1741–1804), Friedrich Wilhelm Joseph von Schelling (1775–1854),[20] and Georg Wilhelm Friedrich Hegel (1770–1831). The line continues to Friedrich von Hardenberg (1772–1801), known to literature by his pseudonym of Novalis, Jean Paul Richter (1763–1825), the Bavarian theosopher Franz von Baader (1765–1841), and *Scenes from the Spirit World* by Heinrich Jung-Stilling (1740–1817), through the physiognomic texts of Johann Kaspar Lavater (1741–1801) and the philosophy of Arthur Schopenhauer (1788–1860). The young Johann Wolfgang Goethe (1749–1832), who had read Swedenborg before he was twenty years old, raised a literary memorial to him in *Faust*, Part II (Act V, Scene 8):

Saved is our spirit-peer, in peace,
Preserved from evil scheming:
"For he whose strivings never cease
Is ours for his redeeming."
I, touched by the celestial love,
His soul has sacred leaven,
There comes to greet him, from above,
The company of heaven.

C. G. Jung records in *Memories, Dreams, Reflections* that he had already read seven volumes of Swedenborg as a young student. But he could scarcely speak to anyone about the profound impression and turmoil that Swedenborg aroused in him: "Hitherto I had encountered only the brick wall of traditional views, but now I came up against the steel of people's prejudice and their utter incapacity to admit unconventional possibilities. I found this even with my closest friends. To them all this was far worse than my preoccupation with theology. I had the feeling that I had pushed to the brink of the world; what was of burning interest to me was null and void for others, and even a cause for dread."[21]

In France, Swedenborg principally influenced Charles Beaudelaire, Gustav Flaubert, Paul Valéry, and Honoré de Balzac. August Strindberg first took note of his famous compatriot at the age of forty-eight after reading Balzac's novella *Seraphita*. Strindberg even dedicated his famous *Blue Book* to the memory of Swedenborg. The influence of Swedenborg on Anglo-American literature extends from Thomas Carlyle, William Blake, William Butler Yeats, Ralph Waldo Emerson, Henry and William James to Elizabeth Barrett-Browning.

Swedenborg's works brought "light into my darkness" for the famous deaf-blind American Helen Keller; her autobiography *My Religion* is first and foremost a tribute to Swedenborg.[22] The Argentinian writer Jorges Luis Borges was familiar with the work of Swedenborg and discussed his work both critically and admiringly. The anniversary volume published for the three hundredth anniversary of Swedenborg's birth gives a wonderful survey of his influence as a natural scientist and visionary.[23] An abundance of bibliographical references make this work a true treasure trove for any one interested in Swedenborg.

Chapter 2

The All-Embracing Whole

The new physics of the twentieth century has confirmed Sweden-borg's view that scientific truth has only limited validity. Science cannot grasp reality in its entirety but always remains an approximation to the truth apparent to human beings. The world does not admit of exhaustive analysis in mathematical formulae and models, as the French thinker and mathematician René Descartes (1596–1650) maintained, whose philosophy so strongly influenced scientific thought. Descartes taught that mind and body are separate. This division of mind and matter led in the following centuries to the assumption that the material universe is a soulless machine, functioning according to strictly deterministic and purely mechanical laws over which man has no influence.

Isaac Newton developed mechanics and classical physics from Cartesian thought, according to which the universe was created and set in motion by God but cannot be influenced further by human intervention.

By contrast, human beings are a creative part of the universe according to the quantum theory elaborated by Max Planck around 1900. Quantum theory proceeds from the assumption that the individual consciousness of a person as observer and participant has a decisive influence on the constantly evolving universe and has helped to form it. This new worldview has completely overturned the mechanistic view of natural science. It is the greatest revolution in the history of science in the modern era. This view of reality arose from the description of things not directly accessible to our senses: the description of atomic and subatomic worlds. However, the quantum theory is scientifically accepted today, and its findings are no longer in any serious doubt.

In actual fact, this worldview is not new at all, but corresponds to ancient teachings, which are being rediscovered by contemporary culture and even natural science today.

All thinking people have posed questions about the origin and nature of the world throughout human history. Both humanists and natural scientists have tried to answer them. Albert Einstein must be one of the most persistent and ingenious of seekers among scientists. He simply wanted to know everything. "I want to know how God created this world. I am not interested in this or that phenomenon, in the spectrum of this or that element. I want to know His thoughts, the rest are details."[1]

The English cosmologist Stephen Hawking is trying to find a "grand unified theory," which will explain why we and the universe exist. It must be comprehensible to all people. For Hawking, the establishment of this complete theory would be "the ultimate triumph of human reason—for then we would know the mind of God."[2]

Fritjof Capra has demonstrated the parallels between modern physics and Eastern mysticism in his book *The Tao of Physics*. Mystics achieve a direct unity with the divine ground of being and thus perceive ultimate reality through personal subjective experience—that is to say, with closed eyes, through surrender and complete absorption. Physicists, by contrast, describe things and try to explain the basic laws of nature and existence through experimental research and measurement. The concept of physics is derived from the Greek word *physis* and originally meant "the endeavor of seeing the essential nature of all things."[3] The accounts of mystics often show startling parallels with quantum physicists' descriptions of reality if compared side by side. This is all the more astonishing because physicists approach reality from an analytical and generally recognized scientific standpoint, while mystics of the ages achieve their insights into reality on intuitive paths. However, unlike the physicists, the mystics need no proofs because they experience the unity of being in their mystical vision and actually perceive the fount of all appearances and thus have true knowledge.

Today's theoretical physicists have found so many new elementary particles in their search for the final building blocks of matter that they have in the meantime given them such labels as "quarks," many of which have a physical property they call "charm." They also use such expressions as the "bootlace principle," "strangeness," or "eight-fold path" behind which the mystery is concealed. Even the language of physics is increasingly changing into a "mystically flavored metaphysics," as Arthur Koestler observed of scientists' difficulties in describing only approximations to physical reality.[4] Theoretical physics can no longer adequately explain and describe the nature and composition of matter in customary language.

Both modes of apprehension—physics and mysticism—are, however, trying to describe a coherent, unified world-picture, in which not even the smallest part can be observed in isolation. Emanuel Swedenborg, who was practicing classical physics in London during Newton's lifetime, anticipated this "new and ancient" world picture in prophetic fashion. The science of his time could give him no explanation of how the world was really constituted. While classical physics was in its infancy and the world was fragmenting into ever smaller parts, each considered independently of the whole, he was already formulating the model of an all-embracing unity, whose description is indistinguishable from that of the unorthodox quantum theoreticians who are seeking the reality behind appearances.

In quantum theory, the universe is considered as an "unbroken whole," in David Bohm's phrase. This unity appears in the atomic and subatomic realms and becomes clearer as one probes deeper into the world of matter. The most varied models of subatomic physics repeatedly show the same unity, namely "that the constituents of matter and the basic phenomena involving them are all interconnected, interrelated and interdependent; that they cannot be understood as isolated entities, but only as integrated parts of the whole."[5] In mysticism, the universe is seen no differently. Its most important characteristic is—as Capra shows—"the awareness of the unity and mutual interrelation of all things and events, the experience of all phenomena in the world as manifestations of a basic oneness. All things are seen as interdependent and inseparable parts of this cosmic whole; as different manifestations of the same ultimate reality."[6] Emanuel Swedenborg describes the universe no differently from an Eastern mystic or a modern quantum physicist. For him, the "universe is a coherent work from first things to last, because it is a work that includes ends, causes, and effects in an indissoluble connection" (*True Christian Religion* 47). "This universal, including its smallest particulars, is a work coherent as a unit, to the extent that no one part can be touched and affected without some sense of it overflowing to all the rest" (*True Christian Religion* 60).

This coherent unity of the universe was confirmed by quantum theory by means of analysis. Quantum theory or quantum mechanics is actually the physics of energy parcels, which Einstein called *quanta* and recognized as a fundamental aspect of nature. Newton's model of a fragmented, mechanistic worldview, according to which all parts of the whole existed independently of one another (that is, as divisible entities) must now be seen as false or only of limited validity on the basis of the new findings of science. The new physics considers the universe as an organism in which not even the smallest part can exist independently of others and the whole. All parts are simultaneously connected with each other and with the whole. The whole and its parts determine one another. Swedenborg also confirmed this in his visionary writings, once he had given up the attempt to find scientific proofs, and stated, "for it is a general rule, that nothing can exist of itself, but from and through something else, consequently that nothing can be kept in form except from and through something else, which may also be seen from everything in nature (*Arcana Coelestia* 6056).

But how is this unified whole, the universe, held together? That is the fundamental question of quantum theory. The procedure for solving this question is so paradoxical that it completely contradicts customary scientific thought. In the mechanistic worldview, all things exist completely independently of the observer, while, in quantum physics, reality is influenced by the observer through the arrangement of his experiment and means of measurement. The result of the observer's investigation *directly* shows exactly what he expects, if only indirectly. "Quantum reality doesn't show up in the quantum facts: it comes indirectly out of the quantum theory, which perfectly mirrors these facts." Or, differently expressed: "Quantum theory, because it precisely mirrors the quantum facts, possesses the same qualities that prevent us from building a consistent observer-free picture of reality from the quantum facts."[7] The results of the physicists are, in the words of Albert Einstein, "free creations of the human mind."[8]

Mystics do not try to prove what they intuitively know, while scientists concede they still do not know what is actually happening in the subatomic realm. The models for their experiments are pure theoretical constructions, and their findings are more experiences than exact results; they rely much more on suppositions concerning what is "real" in this world that is inaccessible to our senses. No one has ever yet seen an atom. However, physicists talk about them as if they are real, although they cannot draw an exact picture of the subatomic world. As Gary Zukav writes in his best-selling classic *The Dancing Wu Li Masters*, "we are so used to the *idea* that an atom is a thing, that we forget that it is an idea. Now we are told not only is an atom an idea, but it is an idea that we cannot even picture."[9] All that is really available to the physicist is the data established at the beginning of an experiment and the results after its completion. What actually happens between these two points, the "variables," is speculation. The only thing that is "real" in the usual sense is simply the multiplicity of measurements, which together form our idea of an atom. The atom itself is never visible.

Since its beginnings, the paradoxes of quantum theory posed not only scientific but also major linguistic problems for the physicist, because they had to describe something, which one could barely conceive. They had to express themselves in a customary language, although none of the concepts really applied. Werner Heisenberg once asked his teacher Niels Bohr whether we might ever really understand the atoms. Bohr replied: "I think we may yet be able to do so. But in the process we may have to learn what the word 'understanding' really means."[10] Quantum physics shows that the structure of nature prevents the simultaneous measurement of two variables. Werner Heisenberg showed this with his "uncertainty principle," which states that the position and impulse of a specific subatomic particle cannot be determined simultaneously, as it can appear both as particle and as a wave. We can always only perceive an aspect of reality. We may measure the momentum or the position of the particle, but never both at the same time. Whatever the observer sees depends on the subjective choice of the observer. If he wants to study the momentum, he arranges his experiment so as to see it. If he wants to determine the position of a particle, he prepares himself accordingly. Reality for the observer depends on his point of view. The great surprise of quantum theoretical research is that there are no perfect methods of measurement in principle, because the experimenter influences the results through his personal perspective. At least this fact is scientifically proven. But no experiment has up until now been able to prove that an observed particle or a quantum (a photon or a quantum of light with zero mass moving constantly at the speed of light) existed before it was observed. The observer appears to be both creator and participant in reality. "Consciousness itself is an intersection of subjective and objective flows."[11] Prior to its observation, the particle only has a "tendency" (according to Heisenberg) to exist. It is so to speak only created and existent through the perception of the observer.

The "dance" of these invisible elementary particles, as the physicists say, hold the whole together. Subatomic events can be measured indirectly only with the most sensitive and complicated instruments of experimental physics through a chain of processes, which end in the clicking of a Geiger counter or as points or traces on a photographic plate. The crucial point is that the phenomena under investigation are never seen but only their effects. "The atomic and subatomic world itself lies beyond our sensory perception."[12]

Meanwhile, physicists shoot particles down ever-larger accelerators, in order to understand their nature. The method seems grotesque because as the size of the accelerators and the energy required increase, the smaller the supposed structures under observation become. They decay into other particles, from which new ones arise. The result is the "cosmic round" (the original title of Capra's *Tao of Physics*) or the "dance of the Wu Li Masters," a living endless process, "because existence is a continual creation, or what is the same, production is continual creation" (*Arcana Coelestia* 3648).

But ever-deeper probing of matter has still not enabled researchers to find the ultimate building blocks of matter. Although new particles are always being discovered and analyzed, the structure of matter is becoming more and more complicated. Quantum physics can confirm an explanation already given by Swedenborg: "Everything divided is more and more manifold, and not more and more simple, because it approaches nearer and nearer to the infinite, in which everything is eternal" (*Conjugial Love* 329).

Swedenborg does not claim this wisdom for himself alone but states clearly: "This concurs with the wisdom of the ancients, whereby all things are divisible without limit" (*True Christian Religion* 33). And he adds, "that everything can be multiplied without end" (*Conjugial Love* 185).[13]

The ancient mystical insight that every part simultaneously contains the whole is exemplified by the holograph, discovered by Dennis Gabor in 1947 (*holo* meaning whole, and *graph* to write). Scientific proof was first possible through the development of laser technology in the 1960s. David Bohm, professor of Theoretical Physics at Birkbeck College, London, explains how the hologram describes the whole, on the one hand, and also shows that every part contains the whole, on the other:

[A holograph is created by] a laser, which produces a beam of light in which the waves of light are highly ordered and regular, in contrast to those of ordinary light where they are rather chaotic. Light from a laser falls on a half-silvered mirror. Part of the waves reflects and part of them comes straight through and falls on the object. The waves that strike the object are scattered off it, and they eventually reach the original beam that was reflected in the mirror and start to interfere, producing a pattern of the two waves super-imposed. It's a very complex pattern, and it can be photographed. Now the photograph doesn't look like the object at all. It may be invisible, or it may look like a vague indescribable pattern. But if you send similar laser light through it, it will produce waves that are similar to the waves that were coming off the object, and if you place your eye in the right spot you will get an image of the object which will apparently be behind the holograph, and be three dimensional. You can move around and see it from different angles, as if through a window the size of the beam.

The point is that each part of the holograph is an image of the whole object. It is a kind of knowledge which is not a point-to-point correspondence, but a different kind. By the way, if you use only a part of the holograph, you'll still get an image of the whole object, but you'll get a less detailed image, and you'll see it from a more limited set of angles. The more of the holograph you use, the more of the object you can see, and the more accurately you can see it. Therefore every part contains information about the whole object. In this new form of knowledge information about the whole is enfolded in each part of the image.[14]

Photography gives only a static record of the light, which is a movement of waves. "The actuality that is directly recorded is the movement itself in which information about the whole object is dynamically enfolded in each part of space, while this information in then unfolded in the image. . . . More generally, movements of waves of all sorts enfold the whole in each part of the universe."[15] If one extracts any given part of the hologram, it will always reflect the whole picture.

Bohm's theoretical model is one of an "implicate" (enfolded) order, which is inherent in the whole universe and which manifests itself by unfolding in the "explicit" order in the apparently separate aspects of time and space. This means that the whole universe is a manifestation of this fundamental order, and that even the smallest particle potentially contains the enfolded complete data of the whole universe. The example of the hologram enables one "to understand intuitively what underlies quantum mechanics."[16] But it is only the "unfolded order" that is accessible to our analysis, from which we can only indirectly infer the "implicate order" in the background. Even if we use only our intellect, we can understand that "the order of the world as a structure of things that are basically external to each other comes out as secondary and emerges from the deeper implicate order. The order of elements external to each other would then be called the unfolded order, or the explicate order."[17] For Bohm, this external order is a consequence of the primary implicate order, in which all things are enfolded in a total wholeness. The fundamental level—that is the third level—that lies behind both these orders is transcendent and not accessible to scientific inquiry. In this way, a quantum physicist has come to the same conclusion as Swedenborg.

According to Swedenborg, the "cosmos" is a "stage" on which all manifestations of the fundamental divine order appear as "witnesses" (*True Christian Religion* 12), but the fundamental order, the actual ground of being and essence, is inaccessible to our senses. Swedenborg gives us a "general definition" of what should be understood by "order," this central concept of his metaphysics: "order is the constitution . . . whose perfection or imperfection follows from the order" (*True Christian Religion* 52).

This ground of being is God, the embodiment of all that is. "God is order, because he is himself substance and form. . . . Everything was good that He created" (*True Christian Religion* 53).

It is interesting that Swedenborg is here trying to define God, although his definition is no definition in the accepted sense. A definition limits what it defines. Here this does not apply because Swedenborg is describing the infinite, which is present in perfect wholeness and inherent in "order." This may be the reason that David Bohm says that he cannot define God and prefers the concept of "implicate" order to express this lack of limitation.[18] Surely, Swedenborg's "definition" of God is to be understood in this sense. This "enfolded" order, the Divine for Swedenborg, is contained in all "unfolded" orders of the universe, just as every part of the holograph contains a complete image of the whole. The order inherent in all things cannot be violated, because it possesses an inner regularity. "God himself cannot act against his divine order because he would be acting against himself in so doing" (*True Christian Religion* 500).

But all manifestations of the secondary order, the structure of things in the whole universe, serve the unity, and every unity serves the order. Thus, the origin—as well as everything that proceeds from it—is always complete because it contains the "implicit"(enfolded) order. Swedenborg states: "We need to bear in mind that everything in the universe, in order to endure, has been created in its proper order—created from the beginning in such a way that it unites with the universal order; this in order that the particular orders may endure in the universal order and so form a single entity" (*True Christian Religion* 54). Moreover: "The wholes behave as the parts and the parts as the wholes in the most perfect form."[19] The "unbroken wholeness" of the universe remains constant.

David Bohm calls the birthplace of the universe the "superhologram," containing everything that is and will be. It is like a "cosmic warehouse" with everything that is, and cannot be conceived in material terms. "It could equally well be called Idealism, Spirit or Consciousness. The separation of the two—matter and spirit—is an abstraction. The ground is always one.[20]

Swedenborg's view and the discoveries of quantum physics that everything proceeds from a spiritual foundation, indeed that the whole world is a manifestation of spirit, is confirmed today both by physicists and representatives of other disciplines. It seems as if the perfect ground of being created humankind as a mirror of itself, although the essence of the absolute always remains unchanged. Swedenborg never says that directly, but we can find a hint when he writes, "The image of the creation is spiritual, but in order to manifest and to create value in the natural world, to establish and persist, it must become matter, it must be composed of the material substances of this world" (*Divine Love and Wisdom* 315).

In quantum physics, this is evident in the apparently chaotic state of elementary particles. The seeming confusion in particle physics, which offers a continual impression of change, destruction, creation, collision, and transformation, is actually based on a wonderful order. Above this dance of particles, "limiting the forms it can take, are a set of conservation laws. They do not specify what must happen, as ordinary laws of physics do, rather they specify what can*not* happen. They are permissive laws."[21] The fundamental inherent order, even in apparent chaos, is always operating in everything, ever since the universe—if indeed it ever had a beginning—was created and which will always exist as long as it remains.

In chaos research, scientists of various disciplines, including mathematics, physics, chemistry, biology, and neurophysiology, are working together to identify the laws behind the apparently chaotic events of the universe. They have concluded that there is neither chance nor disorder, but that apparent fortuitousness and order are inseparable, that simplicity includes complexity and complexity simplicity. The inherent regularity of chaos manifests itself throughout the whole universe. The chaos researchers call this phenomenon a "fractal." The mathematician Benoit Mandelbrot developed the idea of the "fractal" in the 1960s and 1970s. According to the theory, forms that resemble each other repeat themselves infinitely on an ever-decreasing scale, but still retain their original contour. A complexity develops with an incredibly high degree of detail. As in a hologram, every fractal contains the whole.[22]

Meanwhile, scientists have discovered that chaos is by no means a mere confusion but possesses a subtle form of order. According to the researchers, both the simplest orders and the chaos of a system are features of one and the same process.[23] Research has also shown that the path into chaos follows definite rules. As soon as complex systems are investigated, the concept of the part gradually dissolves, with a result that "the scientists of change have learnt that the evolution of complex systems can't be followed in causal detail because such systems are holistic."[24] Until now, no solution could be found for the all-pervading structural principle of the whole universe.

In just a few words, Swedenborg anticipated the complexity of modern chaos research: "Whoever traces effects back to their causes may know that the consistence of all things depends on order. . . . It is this unity that effects the preservation of the whole, which would otherwise fall asunder, and relapse not only into primal chaos, but into nothing" (*True Christian Religion* 679).

Accordingly, an ordering principle is inherent and transcendent in all apparent chaos. Chaos is not some confused random disorder but the absolute fundamental order. But the fundamental level is and remains always untouched by everything that derives from it. Why is this so? Physicists and mystics are trying to answer this question in like manner. Swedenborg answers this question with a comparison, which makes clear how the immutability of the ground of being relates to the world of appearances: "The created world is not God but from God; and because it is from God so it is in his image just as the image of a man is in the mirror in which the man appears but nothing of the man is present" (*Divine Love and Wisdom* 59).

But what transfers the image of the man to the mirror in which his image appears? The great riddle of how man is linked to God and can relate to him is not yet solved. Swedenborg's supreme principle is that everything proceeds from this perfect whole: "Everything comes from the first being/reality and the design has been set up in such a way that the first being/reality is present in its derivatives both indirectly and directly—as present therefore at the end of the design as at its beginning. Only divine truth is substantial—the derivatives are simply forms that come from it in sequence" (*Arcana Coelestia* 7004b). Through this "influence," the Divine is present in everything.

Even David Bohm attempts to explain God extends to limitless being, citing the summons of Moses to whom the voice of God spoke through the burning bush. Bohm is not pursuing theology here but is simply looking at the historical Moses in order to illustrate the difference between limitation and lack of limitation. "When the voice spoke to Moses, it said, 'I am that I am,' and when Moses asked who he should say had sent him unto the children of Israel, the voice replied, 'You shall say, "I am" sent you.'"

Bohm deduces from this story that "I am" is the name of God, because this "I am" is limitless, and there is no inherent property that restricts him. "I am" means to Bohm "universal spirit creating and underlying everything else . . . energy—everything—depends on it; it sweeps all before it."[25] If one was to add a specific property to this "I am," as a woman or man does to assert his ego, he would limit his own being and himself of necessity according to Bohm. Only God is the "self" or the "being," but the individual self and everything that derives from the "self" or "being" in creation is always limited. Swedenborg says, "For what exists in and of itself is the actual being/reality that is the source of everything. Further, being/reality in and of itself is life itself, which is divine love of divine wisdom and divine wisdom of divine love" (*Divine Love and Wisdom* 76).

The whole universe and all its component parts emerge from unity into limitation and simultaneously into polarity. This is true both for man as well as for all other creatures, indeed for all matter. It is one of the chief characteristics of quantum theory. If physicists try to observe the smallest particle ever in isolation, they discover that every particle has a "double nature." It manifests either as a particle or as a wave, as, for example, the photon of light. Light considered as a whole is light; it displays both natures. The smallest unity of light, the photon, can only be observed as a particle or wave in isolation. We find the same principle of apparent duality in Swedenborg. It is a fundamental law and at the same time a decisive sentence in Swedenborg's work, concerning the explanation of the world of appearances: "There is an inner and outer aspect to all creation in the world, be it living or dead. There is never one without the other, just as there is never an effect without a cause" (*True Christian Religion* 595).

However, this apparent duality of each individual part is always a whole or a *holon* (the word coined by Arthur Koestler), because "inner and outer form a whole" as Swedenborg emphasizes (*Arcana Coelestia* 24). These two polar forces are linked in dynamic harmony like the Chinese *yin* and *yang*, simultaneously united and divided. As Swedenborg says, through this polarity of matter and all things of nature, everything is connected and can be linked holistically with the whole, and the same thing applies through the inner constitution of every part howsoever small. David Bohm also says that "a part is intrinsically related to a whole."[26]

Every elemental particle consists of energy and mass. Energy and mass (matter) can transform into one another according to certain laws; they are substance and form, inner and outer. "Mass and energy are different forms of the same thing."[27] The particles distinguish themselves from one another by their special properties, for example, mass, charge (positive or negative), spin (their rotation around their own axis); yet, through their "inner constitution," the "interior" of every particle of matter is somehow linked with the fundamental order. As Swedenborg says in *True Christian Religion* 70, "God is present in the innermost part of the universe and all its separate parts . . . in order to restore order."

In this way, the smallest component particle of the universe contains knowledge of the whole, because the divine is always the same, "in the greatest and the least" (*Divine Love and Wisdom* 79). Nowadays one no longer speaks of material substances in quantum physics but of dynamic "energy bundles," whose structures build up matter and give it the impression of solidity.[28] Accordingly there are no so-called final building blocks of matter. The basic elements are the subatomic particles. These are the vehicles of energy that flow through them, and their structure is their form of vibration determined by their wave nature.

Swedenborg had no sort of measuring instruments at his disposal, by which he could have tested his scientific speculations. However, there are astonishing passages in his scientific writings, in which he describes elementary particles in a manner scarcely distinguishable from that in a modern physics textbook:

> the smaller and closer the parts are to their first simple substratum, the smaller they are in mass, their dissimilarities soften, their imperfections decrease and their forms become more perfect. They are also lighter and quicker in their motion. The more they approach the simple primal substance, the purer they become and they attain the highest perfection in their mechanism and geometry. (*De Infinito* 143)

Here one might compare Capra's comment: "Whenever a particle is confined to a small region of space it reacts to this confinement by moving around, and the smaller the region of confinement is, the faster the particle moves around in it."[29]

Through their special inner properties the individual parts are integrated into an insoluble network of mutual relations, which is constantly changing through their vibrations. For everything in the universe is changed through motion, as Swedenborg already speculated: "When we discuss extended or final things, . . . motion is the cause of all modifications which effect it" (*De Infinito* 136). This is true for the whole universe, as all created things are "final," according to Swedenborg. He had already anticipated the form and nature of wave motion clairvoyantly in his scientific works, although he ostensibly did not yet possess this gift: "The most general and at the same time the most natural form of motion of the elements (that is, the elementary atmospheres) are wave motion . . . and produce through their connection a thousand different movements in the womb of the same continuity" (*De Infinito* 146).

In Swedenborg, the cosmos is always related to human beings, who are in the image of God or the "order," so there is "a complete correspondence between the series of organic elements and the series of cosmic elements: accordingly, the microcosm or human being within his or her limitations resembles the macrocosm within its own" (*De Infinito* 157). Here Swedenborg concurs fully with the teachings of Eastern mysticism. In this passage, he explains the basic principles of the universe as a natural scientist, as he would later find confirmed in his visions.

Through the reciprocity of the particles, everything in the universe is subject to constant change caused by motion. As Gary Zukav has stated, the big question today in nuclear atomic physics is whether the various particles are not simply "different states of motion of some underlying structure or substance."[30]

According to the latest theories of atomic and subatomic physics, it is by no means certain whether there are even "elementary" particles. Physicists speak increasingly of "energy of motion," which can be transformed into mass and thereby conclude that particles are "processes" rather than objects.[31] The particles, even if they exist, convey no energy, but the energy is transformed through their motion. The whole universe is a field of energy. It thus appears "as a dynamic web of inseparable energy patterns."[32] With these assumptions, one can no longer speak of "matter" as it is "actually a series of *patterns out of focus*, really a series of vague patterns. . . . If there is any ultimate stuff of the universe, it is pure energy, but subatomic particles are not 'made of energy,' they *are* energy."[33] The original goal of atomic physics was to find the smallest building blocks of matter. All that the physicists have been able to establish is that there are possibly no building blocks but that everything in the universe is in a state of perpetual reciprocity with corresponding energy fields, whose state is permanently altered by motion. Put in modern terms, one might say, "Everything in the world is pure quantum stuff, a physical union of particle and wave." Or in other words, "the world is one substance."[34]

But paradoxically that substance has a dual nature: particle and wave, matter and energy, or in Swedenborg's terms "substance and form" or "inner and outer." Thus, it can cohere through two "forces" within the atom: through attraction and repulsion. Swedenborg describes these two forces in *Arcana Coelestia* 3628: "There are always two forces which maintain everything in its context and form . . . in whose center the same thing must be whatever is." He is referring to the electrical force of attraction of a positively charged nucleus or the negatively charged electrons, which are drawn as close as possible around it. The electrons react to this spatial limitation by rushing round faster and faster, the closer they are drawn to the nucleus.[35] This gives matter its apparent solidity, which seems all the more solid the faster the movement is that holds the electrons together. This flowing motion is the "basis" that lies behind all appearances, which David Bohm calls "holomovement," as all forms of the material universe spring from it and simultaneously contain the enfolded order. "The holomovement, which is 'life implicit,' is the ground of both 'life explicit' and of 'inanimate matter' and this ground is what is primary, self-existent and universal." The holomovement "carries" the implicate order and is an "unbroken and undivided totality."[36]

Although quantum theory is regarded by physicists as complete, Einstein saw a snag, because quantum mechanics, with whose help the physicists seek to explain the motion of subatomic particles, can only determine its laws statistically (this snag is the essence of quantum mechanics) but cannot precisely predict what will happen to a specific particle according to these laws. Its determinism is limited, as there is no possibility of predicting individual events. Quantum mechanics can only make statements concerning how a certain group of particles will behave. For any individual particle, there are only statements of probability. This means that an individual particle must have, as it were, some freedom of decision. According to the quantum physicists, chance determines however it behaves in a particular circumstance.

This aspect of chance led Einstein to consider quantum theory as incomplete; in his opinion, it did not represent the whole of reality he believed possible. He demanded a theory which would "represent things themselves and not merely the probability of their occurrence."[37] He rejected the assumption that pure chance determines where a photon would strike a photo plate in a so-called double split experiment. He wrote to Max Born: "Quantum mechanics is very impressive but an inner voice tells me this isn't the real McCoy. The theory delivers much but it brings us scarcely nearer to the mystery of God. In any case I am convinced, that he doesn't play dice."[38]

In 1935, Einstein developed an experiment with Boris Podolsky and Nathan Rosen to show the incompleteness of quantum theory. Instead, he unintentionally demonstrated that two particles however far distant from one another are mysteriously connected through a link which transcends our usual ideas of causality. He thus contradicted his own statement that nothing moves faster than the speed of light. This means, in practice, that nothing in the universe is pure chance, as Einstein correctly surmised, but on also that everything must be linked by non-local causes. Einstein did not accept this non-local connection, because it smacked of "telepathy."[39]

But this connection was experimentally confirmed in 1964 by the Irish physicist John Stewart Bell, a specialist in atomic physics. Bell's theorem shows that a pair of photons may begin with the same polarity, but, when they move apart and one alters its polarity through the experiment, the polarity of the other immediately changes. This means that everything is non-locally connected immediately, not through signals that need time for transference. Everything is influenced in each place by an event at another place: it depends on an event at another location, and every local event influences occurrences elsewhere. The physicist Henry Pierce Stapp considers this discovery as "the most profound discovery of science."[40] This also means that it is not "time" that transfers information, but that everything happens simultaneously. A non-local reciprocity connects all places without measuring space, without decay nor delay. It is *unmediated, unmitigated* and *immediate.*"[41] Let us recall again the unified bonding of the whole in Swedenborg: "This all-embracing whole composed of the smallest parts is a coherent single work, that no single point touches and can be excited, without the sensation being transferred to all other parts" (*True Christian Religion* 60).

Even here every single event is momentarily transferred to the whole universe just as Bell's theorem has shown that everything is simultaneously connected. In a reality determined by local events, influences cannot occur with speeds in excess of light, according to the laws of quantum mechanics, because nothing can be faster than light. But Bell's theorem proves that there must be a more profound reality and that our local reality is connected with some basic unity of it. The fundamental unity, inaccessible to our senses, cannot be local, according to Bell, because everything is directly connected and forms a unity. As Nick Herbert writes, "Beneath phenomena, the world is a seamless whole."[42]

With such an assertion, quantum physics comes to the same conclusion as mysticism. Both disciplines complement one another: they are "complementary" as Niels Bohr would say.

But how does humanity relate to this fundamental "seamless" whole? Quantum physics has scientifically solved this fundamental question, so to speak, in its own development. It has provided proof that the consciousness of the observer is a constituent part of the reality under investigation. Human consciousness is, in a manner of speaking, the link between the primary and secondary, or the implicate and explicit, order between the universe and humanity. Without the participation of human consciousness in the ground of being, the absolute being, no collaboration is possible between them. Scientists arrived at this understanding with the discovery of quantum theory. But in so doing, they neglected another essential aspect of reality, the nature of man, who is manifest not only in body and soul but also in unconsciousness and consciousness. Life and consciousness play no role whatsoever in the theories of physics.

It is different for Swedenborg for whom these questions were the only important ones. In the final analysis, his scientific research was a quest for the soul and its seat in the body. In his visionary work, the soul is finally identified as the link with the cosmos, the divine order, which is contained in itself (the microcosm) and enables man to live in accordance with that order and find his wholeness. Order in physics generally means "the interconnectedness of subatomic processes."[43] For Swedenborg, order plays the most significant role in human life, because it is present in the innermost part of the universe and all its separate parts (*True Christian Religion* 70b). This divine order is so perfect that Swedenborg calls it love, a concept that is often used for God today and that finds its most beautiful exposition in *Divine Love and Wisdom* 29:

No one can deny that in God, love and wisdom together are in their very essence. God loves everyone out of the love within him and leads everyone out of the wisdom within him. When we look at the created universe as to its design, it is so full of wisdom from love that you would say everything, taken together, is exactly that. There are countless things in such a pattern, both sequential and simultaneous, that they form a single entity when taken together. This is the only reason they can be kept intact and preserved forever.

Many famous scientists repeatedly posed the question concerning the existence and nature of the supreme power that steers the world. It is frequently assumed that a rational world order exists independently of man, but is not directly apprehensible. The scientist tries to approach God and his world order as closely as possible through the path of induction. That is to proceed from the particular to the general. According to Max Planck, God is always the starting point in the thought of a religious person, while God is always at the end for a scientist. The English mathematician and astrophysicist Sir Arthur Eddington confesses:

We all know that there are realms of the human spirit and the soul which lie outside the world of physics. In our mystical receptivity for the wonders of creation around us, in our artistic expression, in our longing for God, the soul strives to reach higher realms and fulfill something deeply planted within its nature. The justification for this striving lies within us, in a strong urge that awakens simultaneously with our consciousness in an inner light emanating from a higher power than our own. Science can hardly question this inner justification, because its striving springs from an urge, which our spirit must follow, a questioning that cannot be suppressed. Be it in the intellectual striving of science or the mystical longing of the soul, light beckons above and our breast stirs in response.[44]

Even the mathematical reflections of the physicist Burkhard Heim can no longer express reality. For he also admits, "The true nature of life can never be mathematically represented due to its essentially qualitative character." Reflecting on the cause of all existence and the regular patterns of the cosmos, Heim says, "In my view one must ask about the origin of these laws and then conclude that there is an existential reason for the cosmos which lies beyond itself."[45]

The absolute being and its derivative implicit order manifesting in explicit order are the goal of scientific understanding, just as Swedenborg described in his visions.

Natural science is reintroducing metaphysics into the modern consciousness, and in so doing, science once again becomes a humanity. At the end of all its rigorous investigations and proofs, it repeatedly comes to the conclusion that the world is an indivisible whole on the one hand and that it proceeds from a source that is greater than its manifestation, on the other. Pursuing the origin of forms in the material world, the biochemist and cell biologist Rupert Sheldrake has written:

> The universe as a whole could have a cause and a purpose only if it were itself created by a conscious agent, which transcended it. Unlike the universe, this transcendent consciousness would be developing towards a goal; its own goal. It would not be striving towards a final form; it would be complete in itself. If this transcendent conscious being were the source of the universe and of everything within it, all created things would in some sense participate in its nature. The more or less limited "wholeness" of organisms at all levels of complexity could then be seen as a reflection of the transcendent unity on which they depended, and from which they were ultimately derived.[46]

The origin of the universe remains a secret that science cannot explain in Sheldrake's view. His research leads him to conclude that "only faith, love, mystical insight, contemplation, enlightenment, or the grace of God can take us beyond [the limits of conceptual thought]."[47]

According to David Bohm, we are all "manifestations of the

universal. . . . There may be a universal energy pervaded with intelligence and love which is the ground of everything. The real question we should be asking is whether a human being, or group of human beings, can actually come in contact with this universal energy, or be aware of that contact."[48]

Physicists think that consciousness is the intersection of the universe and man. But mystics have always known that everything is consciousness. Even the great physicist and Nobel Prize-winner Erwin Schrödinger tried to answer the final questions through mysticism. He quoted the Islamic-Persian mystic Aziz Nasafi in an essay, in order to illustrate this fundamental unity of consciousness: "Depending on the shape and size of the window, more or less light enters the world. But the light is unchanged."[49]

In Swedenborg, consciousness, "reason," or "outer" is indivisibly linked with the "inner," "love" or "will" of man. Both represent a unity, in order that they can be a part of the whole, a complete "sub-whole" of the cosmic order and thereby a perfect image of the universe. Thus, every single individual is a completely integrated part within a perfect totality. The primal form, from which all forms proceed, is God and human beings are his image, or a representation of the cosmos, of the order. Thus, we are "mirrors" of the universe and will be the center of divine influences. At every point within the universe, we will always be "the centre of divine influences, the image of the heavens is transferred and maps all unto itself" (*Arcana Coelestia* 3633).

Chapter 3

Consciousness

"Science's biggest mystery is the nature of consciousness," writes physicist Nick Herbert, while complaining there is still no theory of consciousness.[1] Meanwhile, quantum physics has scientifically confirmed that physics—indeed all sciences—presupposes the consciousness of an observer. The consciousness of an observer is crucial for the way things are perceived and thus for the findings of science. This very fact was the bombshell of quantum theory. But it cannot explain the nature of consciousness.

What is consciousness, and how does it develop? To what extent is man conscious and what can and should he be conscious of? Swedenborg's visionary work is basically a single answer to this question of all questions, which also subsumes the question of what life is all about. For Swedenborg, every individual consciousness, everything in the created universe, is connected with absolute consciousness or being and a part of this consciousness that is present in all things. Applied to humankind, this means that we are only ostensibly removed from the unity of absolute being, but feel ourselves separated from that which defines our actual essence. As everything in the universe, according to Swedenborg, is love and wisdom, substance and form, inner and outer, and at the same time everything is also a whole or attains to this, then this is also true for the unfolding or development of each individual consciousness. For each person, the unconscious should become conscious. It desires to be integrated into consciousness and so strives towards a wholeness in which it can experience itself consciously as a part of the all-embracing whole and enter into a connection with it.

But what defines the essence of consciousness, and how does it arise? Consciousness proceeds from God who is love and wisdom, life itself and working in the interior of humanity. The consciousness of each individual results from the "love," from the divinity inherent in each person, because this "love" is the divine, "that is, it comes from the Lord alone" (*Divine Love and Wisdom* 399). According to Swedenborg, thought that proceeds from "love" is thus the first effect of life. It should be experienced as conviction, "wisdom," because it determines the life of all people.

Swedenborg's description of this ultimately indefinable love, taken from *Divine Love and Wisdom* 1–2, gives an explanation of what it is, on the one hand, and demonstrates, on the other, its fundamental significance for man:

> Love is the life of man. Man knows that there is love, but he doesn't know what love is. . . . What the life of man is, no one knows unless he knows that it is love. If this is not known, one person may believe that man's life is nothing but perceiving with the senses and acting, and another that it is merely thinking; and yet thought is the first effect of life, and sensation and action are the second effect of life. Thought is here said to be the first effect of life, yet there is thought which is interior and more interior, also exterior and more exterior. What is actually the first effect of life is innermost thought, which is the perception of ends. But of all this hereafter, when the degrees of life are considered.

The "innermost thought," the still unconscious "love," should become the content of conscious being or consciousness in the course of one's life. Love already contains the final intention and goal of the process of individual development and attains its inherent goal by a gradual but ever-increasing dawning of awareness. Everything that pushes forth from this "love," this inner drive into consciousness desires to be lived and realized. The love of each person is his or her inner constitution, the sum of each individual's feelings, through which he or she is linked with the ground of being and through whose special properties that man or woman also consciously relates to everything in the universe through living experience. Love is thus also an impulse, which steers the life of any one person in a particular direction and which wants to find expression as a totality of being. This wholeness is the hidden "final purpose" of innermost thought, already present in the earliest stirring of the soul and consciousness. Love, the innermost propensity, which determines the human essence, leads and steers us towards what we should become and is thereby the content of our true consciousness. "Love" is the fundamental life principle in humans and represents our spiritual form or soul, the organizational principle of our entire life. Everything related to our spiritual realm according to the divine order serves our becoming whole and is perceived by the consciousness as pleasant and harmonious. The inner drive or love is the divine order working in humankind and maintains us in this order. In Swedenborg we read: "All our feelings and thoughts arise from divine love and wisdom" (*Divine Love and Wisdom* 33).

It is quite clear from this wonderful exposition of love and the consciousness arising from it that both have a divine origin and that the essence of true consciousness is divine. The life urge from which love and everything "pleasant" in life proceeds, flows as a stimulus into conscious thought and strives for consciousness and realization. Loving God cannot be meant here in the sense of established religion, but means becoming fully aware of this inner love and inclination, one's own self.

For Swedenborg, consciousness is that which is consciously perceived and thought, "the whole realm of reason or all thoughts of its consciousness" (*Divine Love and Wisdom* 277). To be "wise" from love, consequently, means that thought, "wisdom," must be in harmony with love in order that the order within us may be experienced harmoniously and as a holistic feeling of life. According to Swedenborg, we then feel in "order," in harmony with the cosmos. In the course of our lives, we become increasingly more "self-conscious," whenever we realize the life principle, for "the perfection of life is the perfection of love and wisdom and since our abilities to intend and think are their vessels, perfection of life is also . . . a perfection of our feelings and thoughts" (*Divine Love and Wisdom* 200).

In psychology, one calls this principle "life energy" today, and Stephano Sabetti has outlined a comprehensive model to describe the effects of this energy which strives towards its unfolding in the course of life.[2] In Swedenborg, every individual life and its development stands in a universal context, where it fulfils its assignment of becoming whole at a specific station. Without any theory or needing to produce proofs, Swedenborg simply describes the manifestation of human life and convinces us by the inner logic of his statements in an imagery all his own.

Quantum physics has shown that the whole universe is energy. Today, the physicist Jack Sarfatti goes so far as to say, "that consciousness and energy are one," because they only appear together. He arrives at the same conclusion as Swedenborg, namely that the spirit creates forms and influences matter.[3]

According to Swedenborg, consciousness—spirit—forms the body in a mysterious way and maintains it in a continuous process of transformation. Every thought awakes specific sensations that manifest in the body, called "changes of state" by Swedenborg. The spiritual impulse—the divine—(*Divine Love and Wisdom* 188), which manifests as physical sensation, belongs to a dimension other than physically measurable energy and cannot be demonstrated with ordinary scientific methods. As Swedenborg says, "Thought proceeds from spiritual substances, not from natural substances" (*Divine Love and Wisdom* 257). Accordingly, these spiritual substances must have a different constitution from the natural ones. But how does the spirit or the soul influence the body?

According to Swedenborg, there is a subtle organism in the human body, called the *limbus* or *nexus*, which lacks the mechanical properties of matter. The limbus is the intermediate zone between the physical organism and the supra-sensory soul, "an organizing mold or formative agent serving as the vehicle . . . of forces, . . . conditioned by the soul." The limbus is plastic and assumes any form imagined by the soul. It is the medium "between the spiritual and natural substances.[4] It is most probably a matter of a most subtle or non-material process, which gives rise to the physical effect. Science has not yet been able to explain how this process operates.[5] How consciousness actually works upon the body will probably remain a veiled mystery for sometime.

The spiritual realm manifests itself as an endless stream of consciousness in our thoughts, which assume a spiritual form according to their nature. Swedenborg says, "Love and wisdom are substance and form, likewise feeling and thought" *(Divine Love and Wisdom* 224). Were one to separate instinct and thought from substance, one would destroy them. Love and wisdom are the "carriers" (*subjectum*) of consciousness itself. They are our life energy, the effective divinity within us. "Everything namely, which is still living within man exists in the form of substances, for without these as carriers (of the inner life) they would not exist" (*Heaven and Hell* 418). Swedenborg also calls this instinct the "will," which emerges into consciousness and prevails as the organizing principle of life. "The living striving in man, which is a living form of existence is his will united with reason" (*Divine Love and Wisdom* 219). Everything that emerges from the will and love into consciousness and wishes to become conscious—that is everything which a person loves and feels attracted to—determines existence and demands to be lived.

David Bohm calls the content of consciousness "meaning," which inheres in energy and is unfolded by it. The content of consciousness also determines man's being for Bohm:

Conscious awareness, its essential feature, is meaning. The content that one is consciously aware of, is meaning. And that meaning is active. The activity of consciousness is determined by the meaning. Therefore you could say that consciousness, both in the features that we experience and in its activity, is meaning. Without meaning there is no consciousness. And the greater the development of meaning, the greater the consciousness . . . if meaning is what life is—then a change of view of meaning is a change of life.[6]

Body and spirit form a unity, but Swedenborg says what is decisive is that "the body can do nothing by itself, only through the spirit inherent in it" (*Divine Love and Wisdom* 401 [i]). Every individual thought works momentarily upon the form of the body and matter. Body and spirit are inseparably connected with each other. David Bohm also says, "Purpose flows out of meaning, and through the action carried out, the meaning further changes, and we are back in the cycle."[7] Here we find the famous motto of esotericism: "we are what we think" in the statement of a scientist.

"We are, what we think. Everything that we are arises from our thoughts. We make the world with our thoughts." Gautama Buddha taught this. This magical sentence can be found today in almost all books on positive thinking and in esoteric literature. Often the reader is told that one can be anything that one thinks. One has only to visualize one's desired aim, and the unconscious will start to realize the goal. This insight of realizing one's goal was written down by Swedenborg more than two hundred years ago: a human being can realize everything, that he or she can imagine—by all means on the plane of pure thought, as thoughts are independent of time and space. We find him saying: "man can make manifest whatever he directs his thoughts upon with concentrated attention" (*Heaven and Hell* 196).

Many of today's "psychotechnicians" abuse esoteric traditions and actually assume in their training that one can correct one's direction in life whenever one wishes through influencing the unconscious and altering the content of one's thoughts. "Mind over matter" is nowadays a state-of-the-art psychological tool to motivate anyone hitherto unaware of his or her spiritual powers towards achievement within the space of a few days or weeks. Many writers on positive thinking and so-called mental training make this assumption. The principle is simple: one assumes that spirit trains matter. The power of imagination is also emphasized because it creates spiritual images, which are supposed to achieve the desired goal, often with no reference to ethical concerns, social constraints, and individual limitation. "Success" is nowadays regarded as a materially visible and measurable result, rather than a spiritual achievement and ethical act, which is a private matter.

Western esotericism teaches that thought influences forms and fashions our reality. "Our state of consciousness is the impulse which allows energy takes on this or that form."[8] As every form of energy in the whole universe has a specific form, so does every single thought have its characteristic form. So Swedenborg teaches: "All tendencies and thoughts of people are in forms, and therefore from forms, for the forms are the carriers of the same tendencies and thoughts" (*Conjugial Love* 186).

The theosophists Annie Besant (1847–1933) and Charles Webster Leadbeater (1847–1934) were convinced that the characteristic shape, form and color of thought forms are determined by the nature of the corresponding thought.[9] But only the power of the will produces the necessary energy to realize thoughts. As a natural scientist, Swedenborg had already speculated on the ways in which consciousness has a transforming effect upon the body. His surmise that the spiritual impulse is transferred by "emotion" is hardly disputed today, and so his description of the conversion of energy seems utterly modern: "When activated by virtue of their inclusion in an organism, the waves and vibrations form the 'animal spirits' in the truest sense, which obey the stirrings of the soul and realize everything simultaneously desired by body and soul" (*De Infinito* 154).

Superficially considered, these lines read like a patent recipe for every "trainer" selling "spiritual fitness." Accordingly, we need only tune in to the desired wavelength, clearly visualizing our goal, in order that our thoughts may provide sufficient impetus for their actual realization by the power of our consciousness. But it is not that simple. In this recipe, scarcely any consideration is given to the innate psychic structure of the person. Positive life changes or even long-term success are not possible without taking into account the innermost disposition. A mere external dose of new "thought forms" cannot make new people, without taking account of the inner "love" and "disposition," as well as individual potential and challenges. Swedenborg says expressly, "If man is left to himself, he rejects everything which does not accord with his love" (*New Jerusalem and Its Heavenly Doctrine* 113). We cannot just be manipulated indefinitely. For example, we cannot have a successful career in the long run, unless we follow our personal disposition, our innermost love. Only the person who chooses his or her activity from innermost propensity and acts accordingly can be successful and carry great burdens in his or her career. If we act contrary to our inner conviction and innermost belief, which is not always even conscious, the most ingenious training program will not function. But: "Whatever is the object of a dominant love, is loved above all. What man loves above all, is continually in his thoughts because it is present in his will and represents his very own life...because man is so created like the dominant principle of his life" (*True Christian Religion* 399).

This "dominant" inner principle of life always presses to prevail because it strives for completion and wishes to be realized in the outer world. It is the pressure for the realization of the Self, it is the—mostly unconscious—original motivation behind every action.

Most people are completely unaware why they do what they do; they frequently do the right thing or the wrong thing unconsciously, driven by their tendencies, which act as their inner motor and produce thoughts that lead to action. With closer consideration and consciousness of one's action, each one of us would probably realize what we can read in Swedenborg: "Whoever pays attention, can discern that every thought proceeds from a tendency . . . and every idea is ensouled and enlivened by a tendency" (*Heaven and Hell* 236).

But the "level" of consciousness and its "constitution," the quality, negative or positive nature, of "love" and its resulting thoughts are crucial for the consequence of our action. This "love," which determines the life of each human being, is expressed in the endless multiplicity of feelings and tendencies from which human actions proceed, and therefore always gives an indication concerning "intentions," with which each thought is associated. All people must judge these in critical self-examination according to the best of their knowledge and conscience, before they come to light as an act. Swedenborg's guide to this examination of conscience sounds so obvious and illuminating that one would think that they would be universally accepted: "The spirit cannot be investigated other than by man taking note of his thoughts especially his intentions for these are the thoughts of the will and here is evil in its origin and root, i.e., in his carnal appetites and desire" (*Divine Providence* 152). Or in other words: "it is the job of a wise man to recognize his own intentions . . . to recognize, from which source the tendencies come!" (*Arcana Coelestia* 3796). "We have a freedom to think as we wish, to the end that our life's love may come out of hiding into the light of understanding; . . . otherwise we would know nothing of our evil side, and would not escape it" (*Divine Providence* 281).

The "love" of man contains, whenever it is unrealized innermost thinking, the properties most positively associated with it, and every single degree of negative will and its associated "evil," which works simultaneously on positive intentions as well as on the spiritual unconscious context. Individual responsibility begins with the will and thinking, and with responsibility comes the free will and self-determination of consciousness of all human beings. For thoughts do not simply expire; they retain their reality and effect on a spiritual plane and influence everything connected similar in form. For example, Swedenborg saw and described his visions more than two hundred years ago. However, this fact of absolute intercommunication has only become topical and a matter of general awareness today through the notable books of Rupert Sheldrake concerning "morphogenesis," the genesis of forms in the organic and inorganic realms of the whole universe.

Sheldrake contrasts his theory concerning the reciprocity of spirit and matter in the "hypothesis of formative cause" with materialist thinking. Besides the force fields known to physics, there are "morphogenetic fields"—one could equally well call them spiritual fields—serving the generation and transformation of characteristic forms on both mental and material planes and also manifesting themselves in human behavior.

It follows that a "formative cause" antedates all existing material forms as well as all developments in the intellectual history of mankind and individuals in the whole universe. This cause is non-energetic and thus not physically measurable. It is the implicit impulse, inherent in all forms of the whole universe in their endless multiplicity, and allows them to unfold their final form. All forms of matter, from the smallest to the greatest and most complex, from the proton and crystal through the kingdom of plants to man, have morphogenetic or morphic fields that always work from the higher plane to the next one below and thus coordinate the arrangement of parts and the generation of form. The morphic fields are "hierarchically packed" in their organization and contain complete information on all past history and evolution. All existing forms are subject to the influence of similar forms in the past. They are connected with another through "morphic resonance," which is effective over time and space with no delay and is thereby analogous to the non-local references of quantum theory.

Morphic resonance means that "the form of a system, including its characteristic internal structure and vibrational frequencies, becomes *present* to a subsequent system with a similar form; the spatio-temporal pattern of the former *superimposes* itself on the latter."[10] Morphic resonance is stronger the more similar the morphic field or an organism is to its predecessor. The "transmission" from earlier similar systems is made, while "reception" depends on the corresponding organization and structure of the receiver. The influence of morphic resonance remains constant, independent of time and space and occurs in all similar morphic fields. The past is as it were "impressed" on the present.[11] A morphic field can only influence systems tuned to itself, namely, where resonance is present.[12]

Sheldrake's hypothesis can be applied to all aspects of human behavior and learning abilities. All learned behavior is transferred from one organism to the other, which wants to acquire this special behavior without the need for a model. The more often specific behavior recurs, the stronger and more stable will be the resonance and the more pronounced the respective pattern of behavior or thought.

To Swedenborg, everything in the universe has a spiritual cause, which according to its inner form acquires a corresponding outer form in the material world, analogous to morphic fields. Thus, the "spiritual form" or the "spiritual shape" of a human being, which is both "form and substance," fashions the corresponding form of the body, which is both "substance" and "form." The same is true for the influx of conscious content, which induces inner perception. According to Swedenborg, thoughts hover in the "heavenly aura— similar to notes in the air and ripple out like waves" (*True Christian Religion* 173 [b]).

As Swedenborg was already trying to show speculatively in his scientific works, that everything is linked by vibrations, he had also grasped the general principle that every "resonator" is simultaneously a "transmitter."[13] All thought forms produce vibrations, which evoke "sympathetic" vibrations in similar thought forms and thereby awaken thoughts of the same type as those transmitted by the spirit of the originator. "Man sees and feels according to the form of these inner things and their harmony" (*Heaven and Hell* 351).

"Because the will and reason are the vessels of love and wisdom they are both organic form; . . . how else could thought cohere and how could one talk out of thought if it were not coherent?" (*Divine Love and Wisdom* 373).

Both the spiritual form and the form of the body change with every perception, every thought, every intention, every stirring of the will, or, in Sheldrake's words, every morphic unity which envelops each living creature. "For," says Swedenborg, "there are no changes of state without substantial form as their vehicles, just as there is no seeing without an eye and no hearing without an ear" (*Divine Love and Wisdom* 273), because there is no substance without form (*Divine Love and Wisdom* 209). "Will and reason," "instinct and thought" are "conditions of substances and form . . . just like the sensations and actions, which are not derived from the sensory and motor organs" (*Divine Love and Wisdom* 210).

Swedenborg repeatedly described in his visionary work how the spirit works on the body and how all changes in the body are caused by perception. For people are, above all, "spiritual figures," to whom the "inner world" lends form. Humanity is linked through the inner world to the whole cosmos, in morphic resonance to use Sheldrake's words. Each human being is connected with every other human being and thereby subject, consciously or unconsciously, to all good and evil influences. A man can influence all corresponding thoughts and tendencies through his thinking and willing (or morphic field), because he is the center of all influence both as "transmitter" and as "receiver." According to Sheldrake, every individual "inherits" the collective characteristics of all people with the morphic fields under whose influence we stand, as the "structures of thought and experience that were common to many people in the past" condense into morphic fields through morphic resonance. Sheldrake compares this inheritance of humanity with C. G. Jung's concept of "collective unconscious," whose contents are not in individual consciousness but are inherited and whose influence underlies the content of each.[14]

Thus, every individual codetermines the history of humankind in a negative or positive sense either unconsciously or consciously, and every individual will collaborate further in history through his or her thoughts and the level of individual consciousness. Our greatest responsibility for all living things and everyone who comes after us lies in this phenomenon.

According to Sheldrake, every characteristic form has a morphogenetic field, which already contains the final form—for example, a specific plant or the adult shape of a rabbit—in its unfolding material form and dictates its development. This means it already contains the "potential" state of developing system before its final form has arisen. "At the end of a process of morphogenesis, the actual form of a system comes into coincidence with the virtual form given by the morphogenetic field."[15]

Human beings are similarly determined by a goal corresponding to their spiritual form and inner structure and are steered towards this goal by the "inclination of innermost thought," their "love." According to Swedenborg, "purpose, cause and effect" follow according to the order, "like earlier, later and final." The "final purpose"—that is, the goal—produces the effect through the cause, "in order that the final purpose may manifest" (*Divine Love and Wisdom* 189). The only question is to what extent we play an active role or not regarding the intended goal, which is attributed to us.

Sheldrake's "hypothesis of formative causation" is valid in any event only for the "repetition" of forms, that is, for the continued existence and development of already existing forms, while the origin of continually new forms and patterns of organization remain mysterious and cannot be explained by known scientific methods. Sheldrake asserts that morphogenetic fields are not material in a specific sense. Scientists cannot pronounce on their nature or origin or on what determines each individual form for the first time. According to Sheldrake, the question of the origin of morphogenetic fields can only be answered on the basis of metaphysics.[16] By asking this question, Sheldrake comments:

> We find ourselves in the presence of several long-established traditions of thought about the ultimate creative source, whether this is conceived of as the One, Brahma, the Void, the Tao, the eternal embrace of Shiva and Shakti, or the Holy Trinity. In all these traditions we sooner or later reach the limits of conceptual thoughts, and also at a recognition of these limits.[17]

As a natural scientist, Swedenborg could not answer the question of immaterial origin any better. But as a metaphysician, he gave a detailed explanation:

Everyone who thinks from clear reason, also sees that everything is created from one substance, which is substance in itself; for this is itself the Being, from which everything that is has its existence. And because God alone is substance in himself and thus the Being itself, it is clear that no where else lies the existence of things. (*Divine Love and Wisdom* 283)

From this one can clearly see, that the divine, which is substance in itself or the one and only substance, is the same thing from which each and everything created has its being, so that God is all in everything of the universe. (*Divine Love and Wisdom* 198)

The visionary Swedenborg gives the answer whence the uninterrupted creativity of the universe comes, in which there is an endless multiplicity of forms of which none resembles the other. Natural science can no more answer this question than the question of the origin of all things. How, for example, does a new idea arise, a new thought or a new morphic field? Sheldrake denies that the origin of this mysterious event can be explained solely by past events. "New fields start off as insights, intuitive leaps, guesses, hypotheses or conjectures. They are like mental mutations. New associations or patterns of connection come into being suddenly by a kind of 'Gestalt-switch.'"[18]

Even Swedenborg doubts we can investigate the innermost ground of our thinking. We encounter only the finished thought, idea, or inspiration flashing into our consciousness. Swedenborg hints at this experience: "The tendencies of inner thought . . . from which the outer ones proceed are never clearly presented to people's eyes; . . . if you could see just one concept opened up, you would see incredibly more than the tongue could tell" (*Divine Providence* 199). The expressive capacity of language faces insurmountable barriers in explaining the ineffable. Even mysticism circumscribes the true, which can never be appropriately expressed in words.

As a natural scientist, Rupert Sheldrake poses all the questions that the mechanistic worldview cannot answer. They are the same questions that Swedenborg wanted to ask of the natural sciences in his era. In the inner coherence of his visionary work, Swedenborg answers all the basic questions concerning the meaning and coherence of the universe that remain a riddle to scientists today, despite the enormous progress of the last two hundred years.

Still unexplained, for example, is the mystery of the "quantum leap" in physics, which occurs completely abruptly and signifies an unpredictable transition of an elementary particle into another state. According to Sheldrake, the phenomenon of a new morphic field signifies likewise a "leap" or a "discontinuity." As all morphic fields like all individual things in the universe—be they material forms or new ideas—are always wholes and indivisible; they must manifest apparently all of a sudden. "New patterns include old ones within themselves; nevertheless they are new and come into being suddenly; they have a wholeness and integrity that do not admit of gradual appearance."[19] In fact, countless inner effects precede this apparently sudden transition into a new form, but they do not manifest outwardly. Swedenborg gives an example of the unconscious events in the spiritual nature of man in *Conjugial Love* 185:

> The changes that take place in our internal being are more perfectly continuous than those which occur externally, for that reason our internals, by which are meant the things of our minds or spirits, are in a higher degree, elevated above our externals; and in the things that are in the higher degree thousands of changes take place in the same moment that one occurs in externals.

Swedenborg explains the manifestation and multiplicity of these "wholes" through an equally great multiplicity of developmental stages, which he describes as "grades"(or levels), which are in every whole—he calls them "love and wisdom," "substance and form," or "inner and outer"—and always manifest simultaneously as a whole. Like the quantum leap, the transition from one grade or from one developmental stage to the next represents a passage from one state to another and thus a new quality. They behave towards one another rather like a new morphic field belongs to an earlier one:

> There are two types of levels . . . increase and decrease...as from light to darkness or from warmth to cold, . . . [and] distinct levels, . . . like end, cause, and effect. These latter levels are called distinct because the first exists in and of itself, as do the second and the last; yet they form a single entity when taken all together. (*Divine Love and Wisdom* 184)

These two types of grades are to be found in everything throughout the whole universe: "in the greatest and in the smallest things" (*Divine Love and Wisdom* 236).

According to Sheldrake, there is not even one form which is identical to another. Swedenborg explains why this is so: "Since there are these levels in things greatest, with corresponding distinctions from top to bottom and from center to circumference, it follows that there are not lesser or least components . . . that are identical." (*Divine Love and Wisdom* 226).

According to Sheldrake's hypothesis of formative causation, all "structures of activity" in the whole universe, whatever their size, have their own morphic fields:

> It makes sense to think of the entire universe as an all-inclusive organism [and] if so, then by analogy with all the kinds of organism within it, the entire universe would have a morphic field which would include, influence, and interconnect the morphic fields of all the organisms it contains. If such a universal field exists, its properties and structure will be shaped by morphic resonance. . . . The universal field will be subject to morphic resonance from its own past states, most specifically from the immediate past, but going right back to the beginning. This self-resonance would help to explain the continuity of the universe, as well as the continuity of material systems within it.[20]

Sheldrake's hypothesis was already a fact for Swedenborg.

Thus, nothing in the universe can "arise and exist without ordering itself within a collective" (*Arcana Coelestia* 42). The key to this collective subordination lies once again in Swedenborg's doctrine of the grades. Parallel to Sheldrake's hypothesis, all grades with Swedenborg are ordered in a "packed hierarchy," in which each new or later form contains the "memory" of all preceding forms. "One must know," says Swedenborg, "that every grade is separated from the other by means of its own envelopes and all grades together are distinguished by means of a common envelope and that the common envelope is connected with the inward and inmost in its order, as a result of which the connection and illuminating effect of all things occurs" (*Divine Love and Wisdom* 194). "The first grade is all in everything of the following grade. . . . The first grade is all in all of the following grades" (*Divine Love and Wisdom* 195).

Just as, according to Sheldrake, each new form or every new morphic field contains complete information about all preceding forms, the same is true for Swedenborg: "The last grade is the conclusion, the container and foundation of preceding grades" (*Divine Love and Wisdom* 209). It contains all earlier forms and so contains the continuity of all existing things and the universe itself.

But Sheldrake's hypothesis of formative causation relates not only to the origin of material forms but equally to the entire history of the human spirit that derived from a unified immaterial common spirit, which then took form in the development of different arts, cultures, religions, and sciences. The mutual inspiration of various schools, one on the other, consists in this "in-fluence" of formal, stylistic and spiritual elements. Morphic resonance is a plausible explanation for this exchange between various traditions, but also for continuity and heritage within each tradition. "They are supra-individual fields, and have a life or spirit or atmosphere of their own."[21]

According to Swedenborg, everything spiritual and material in the universe is subject to the influence of a superior whole, which he once again justifies with his doctrine of the grades:

The largest thing in which the grades of both types are found is the universe in its whole extent . . . ; the smallest is the individual person . . . , the animal, the tree . . . ; the Divine out of which they are created is the same in the largest and the smallest. (*Divine Love and Wisdom* 225)

The Divine fills all spaces of the universe independently of space, we are told in *Divine Love and Wisdom* 69. The Divine dwells "in each and every thing of the created universe" (*Divine Love and Wisdom* 60):

Out of the Uncreated, Eternal, Being itself and Life itself, no one can be directly created, because the divine is one and indivisible; rather it must be made from created and mortal substance, so formed that the divine can dwell within it. (*Divine Love and Wisdom* 4)

This Divine is nothing other than consciousness, because it possesses the total knowledge of the all-embracing whole in all individual parts of the universe and thereby steers the shaping of individual forms towards their goal and their destiny within the whole. Rupert Sheldrake similarly thinks a unified theory concerning the origin and explanation of the universe including organic life and consciousness is of paramount importance.[22]

Swedenborg wrote thousands of pages in order to give us a clue of how the divine, "love," from which "inclination" proceeds, is always coincident with "wisdom" and consciousness and pervades the whole universe. One can never express in chemical or mathematical formulae this "substance," which is simultaneously form and vehicle (*subjectum*) and carries all knowledge in itself. The divine being, God, is also the *self*, contained in everything that is, because God is life, love, and wisdom: "If these did not make up the Self in God, they would exist neither in heaven nor earth . . . thus the omnipresence of God" (*True Christian Religion* 25).

There is a parallel passage in the Upanishads: "The Soul is Brahman, the Eternal. It is made of consciousness and mind: it is made of life and vision. It is made of earth and the waters: it is made of air and space. . . . It is made of all that is near: it is made of all that is afar. It is made of all."[23]

We are linked with the divine, the omnipresence of God, the spirit or cosmic consciousness through our limitless and limited self, which, according to Swedenborg, is both substance and form, love and wisdom. And our spirit shapes our body, which is permanently changed through the constant stream of consciousness from within to without and vice versa. Because there is an "inner" and an "outer" or "love and wisdom" in all created things of the world and everything in the universe is conscious, the conscious field of each human being and his or her link with the cosmos proceed from within because everything is linked with the whole from the inwards out.

The more a man or woman becomes a "vessel of God," in modern parlance a receptacle of cosmic consciousness, which she *is* according to Swedenborg, the more she expands her individual consciousness, which is as infinitely creative as the expanding universe.

> The eternity of God can manifest to an illuminated reason on the basis of that eternity, unto which every science, and consequently man's insight and wisdom can expand, because both, insight and wisdom, can grow like a tree from its seed. . . . They recognize no boundaries. The memory of man is their soil, they germinate in the intellect and bring their fruits forth in the will. Both faculties, intellect and reason, are so constituted that they are educated throughout our mortal span and can be completed in eternity. (*True Christian Religion* 32)

Through our feelings and thoughts, through the ceaseless stream of consciousness, we are both a sounding board and receiver, as well as a transmitter, continually linked with the universe and the divine origin and simultaneously co-creators or spoilers of the spirit that expands from our center. Our creativity and generative powers express themselves in every thought and go on working quite independently of time and space on the spiritual plane corresponding to one's level of consciousness. The person who is unaware of this fact—in Swedenborg's parlance, "the natural man"—may conclude that "he would be deprived of all thought if the ideas of time, space, and material things were taken away; for upon these all the thought of man rests; however, the soul is projected over material and mundane things" (*Heaven and Hell* 169).

We are all continually linked through our personal inner spiritual structure, our own "morphic field," with corresponding fields of consciousness and are simultaneously influenced by them, even if we are unaware of it. Swedenborg describes this mutual influence frequently with examples from the "spiritual world" in which there are no limits to consciousness and every thought is perceived in the blinking of an eye. According to its nature, "every thought of his intellect and every stirring of his will spreads out into the heavens . . . although he could scarcely think of anything without this light" (*Heaven and Hell* 203).

Through our inner worlds, we are united with the spiritual world and influenced by it, just as we conversely influence cosmic events through our feelings, desires, and thoughts. Each person must become aware of his or her place in this unity and its consequences. The certainty that every thought lives on a higher or lower plane of reality simultaneously signifies the enormous responsibility connected with our thinking. The "spiritual deed" endures even if no material deed directly succeeds it. Therefore, humanity must always be aware of this responsibility concerned with our thoughts and desires and steer each thought in the right direction. Human beings are responsible for their acts through the gift of free will, even if the causes of events are often to be sought in the outer world of social or political circumstances or merely in the immediate environment. Every individual helps create the world through his or her thoughts.

Everything that a person has ever thought is contained in his or her spiritual body, even if this form constantly changes throughout life and is transformed by the development of consciousness. We are responsible for our thoughts; indeed, we determine our own "Last Judgment" even while living: "Everything that a man hears and sees—all that he has ever thought, spoken, and done, from earliest infancy to the last of old age—the memory of all these things—this is the book of his life, which is opened in the other life and according to which he will be judged" (*Arcana Coelestia* 2474). Swedenborg even says: "Whatever is in [the book] can never be erased. . . . Each and everything will be apparent as in the clear light of day" (*Heaven and Hell* 463).

Once one has grasped this conception in its full implications, this knowledge will gradually work on all conscious thinking, while one tries to think more responsibly. The idea that every evil intention and the contents of our minds will be etched in our spiritual body, which survives death, might warn many people to be more attentive and careful in their thinking. But even this kind of rethinking would still be too straightforward and shallow, as it would correspond to "outer thought" or the "lower ego," which only considers punishment and selfish motives rather than authentic feeling and inner conviction. People should realize their inner form, the truly divine in each of us, which is our real essence. According to Swedenborg, the sense and purpose of every individual life is to live out his God-given love of life contrary to any negative influence from without and to fulfill completely our appointed place in creation. The divine guide within leads each person to what he or she should become. This is also the teaching of the *Bhagavad Gita* (xvii, 61-62):

A Master dwells within all creatures,
He has his throne in the human heart
By his will he leads men
Towards the Good. His will is law.

Find sanctuary in him, your salvation;
To him, utterly surrender your soul;

By His grace you will obtain peace,
Blessedness of supreme existence.[24]

We should listen to this inner divine guide in order to achieve our inner form. This actually demands great exercise of self-control and discipline and is a never ending struggle for the inner to prevail over the outer. Swedenborg's advice to set off on the "inner path" sounds very simple and illuminating; but, in reality, it is a lifelong conflict between inner and outer which is consciously undertaken by the reversal of outer and inner and the discovery of the inner world. As he states in *Heaven and Hell* 351, "The only means to educate the inner world consists in man directing his gaze towards the Divine and heaven. . . . It should be clear enough what true insight and wisdom are."

In the discovery of the inner world, the only true expansion of consciousness, the development of the intellect and the accumulation of externally acquired knowledge are only secondary. The primary concern is the "unfolding of visionary sight," in the words of Inge von Wedemeyer.[25] This "inner sight" approaches a mystical experience that allows us to recognize the essence of things from within and gives a feeling of concord. People of the West should try to walk this path with the aid of a teacher and spiritual instruction, in common with the religious practice of the East. Once one is aware of the necessity of this inner guidance, there is a decisive turning point in life, the conversion of the hitherto outwardly directed person, who was not yet aware of inner guidance and the immanent divine. For each person only needs to become his or her "inner self," in order to fulfil his role in creation. The path is long and hard, a life-long process of transformation that Swedenborg called the "spiritual rebirth," which proceeds from one's intention to become what one should become: a mirror of his or her most profound actual inner world—thus, the image of God.

Chapter 4

Spiritual Rebirth

The occult nature of Swedenborg's visionary writings lies in his exegesis of the inner sense of the Bible, especially the first book of Moses. He questions the dogma of the Christian church but indicates the unifying principle of all the great world religions: there is only one God and Creator with whom all people are connected. According to Swedenborg, "no mortal can understand the Bible nor Genesis literally, because the 'literal sense' does not allow one to apprehend anything besides the Old Testament's general reference to the external history of the Jewish church. But everywhere there is an inner sense which does not manifest itself outwardly" (*Arcana Coelestia* 1).

Swedenborg analyzes the seven days of creation as the "stages of man's becoming," which man has to ascend in order to be united with God and become his image. It is a lifelong process of development in soul and spirit, concerned with the unfolding of "inner" or "spiritual" vision, the intuitive soul faculty and, with it, the training of various levels of consciousness, and the discovery of the inner world. This links man with the divine or cosmic true consciousness and allows him to participate in it according to the unfolding and ripening of his inner world.

The seven days of creation are identical with the training of the seven centers of consciousness in the Eastern doctrine of the chakras. Swedenborg calls them "the new creation of man" or the "spiritual rebirth" (*Arcana Coelestia* 1), which proceeds from humanity's recognition of our link with God to the phased discovery of the inner world. Divinity in humankind is, according to Swedenborg, closed at birth but progresses through a continual process of transformation, a conflict between inner and outer, until the end of one's life. The deeper one explores the inner world, the higher one's consciousness is raised and the more inward the union with God and the visionary sight beyond material manifestations. "The connection with the Lord and regeneration are one and the same" (*Divine Providence* 92).

In the last analysis, it is a matter of returning to paradise, lost by humans when they acted contrary to the commandment of God: "You may eat indeed of all the trees in the garden. Nevertheless of the tree of the knowledge of good and evil you are not to eat, for the day you eat of it you shall most surely die" (Genesis 2:16–17).

Through this "Fall," we have lost our inner mystical link with God and sealed the source of true perception that comes alone from "inner vision," which the people of the early church still possessed. By "church" (Greek, *kyrikon*, derived from *kyriakos*, "belonging to the Lord," *kyrios*), Swedenborg means neither historical confession nor institution. He is concerned with the individual as a "vessel" and thus as a dwelling place of God, which works within each person as the sole source of true consciousness and knowledge. "The men of the early church received their experience of true faith through revelations for they talked with the Lord and angels and were taught by visions and dreams which were utterly wonderful and blissful and perceived as good and true when anything false presented itself, they not only avoided it but regarded it with horror" (*Arcana Coelestia* 125). Today, we call these wonderful states of consciousness heightened, expanded, or transpersonal. Their mystical vision, a vision completely undimmed by outer and material thinking, explains the mystery of true perception and belief, which comes only from a perfectly profound experience, the "remembrance" of things in themselves, their perception in their complex totality. According to Swedenborg, this "remembrance" is a certain inner feeling, an inner perception of truth and goodness, a feeling that radiates only from the Lord" (*Arcana Coelestia* 104). Only then is humanity linked with the divine ground of being, the true consciousness, and released from our acquired outer knowledge and the sensory deception of the material world. Swedenborg describes the "inner" (spiritual) and "outer" (material) thought as follows:

> Thinking spiritually means thinking about things in themselves; to see truths in the light of truth, and to perceive goods from the love of good; also, to see the quality of things. But to think materially is to think, see, and perceive them together with matter, thus in a gross and obscure manner respectively. (*New Jerusalem and Its Heavenly Doctrine* 39)

Countless veils obscure the true fundamental reality, whose aspects manifest in endless variety in the world of matter, but do not allow the true essence to become visible. Thus, the "outer man" is subject to the deception of his senses, which he takes for reality, while the ground of his being remains hidden; he can only experience and believe this through an inner revelation. Therefore, Swedenborg says that all people "should seek to investigate the mysteries of faith by means of every perception derived from the Lord but not from self and the world" (*Arcana Coelestia* 126–127).

> The more a man seeks to be wise [on the basis of his senses], the more he is blinded until he believes nothing, not even that there is anything spiritual, or that there is eternal life. This comes from the principle which he assumes. . . . This is eating from the tree of knowledge of good and evil, and the more he eats from this tree the more lifeless he becomes.

Everyone can recognize that the principles we adapt—no matter how false—guide us. . . . If our basic principle is not to believe anything until we see and grasp it, there is no way for us to believe. . . . The true order is . . . to gain wisdom from [the Lord's] Word. . . . We must start from the Lord, not from ourselves. The former is life; the latter, death. (*Arcana Coelestia* 128–129)

The "own" is what we commonly call the "self." It is self-deception, which arises through sensory perception and our rational thought; indeed, it is the totality of impressions that seem to make up our lives. But it is by no means divine knowledge or divine will ("Lord, Thy will be done!") that ensouls us from within but only that which a man believes he can and wants to do on the basis of his lower ego and emotions. "The own consists in all evil and falsehood, which bubbles up from love of the self and the world and from supposing that what cannot be apprehended sensuously and by means of memory-knowledge is nothing" (*Arcana Coelestia* 210). This lower ego or the "human self" should be overcome by spiritual development in order to unite with the truly Divine and so attain the goal of human destiny: "The own of man is *his* will. . . . Therefore, no one can be blessed who allows himself to be led by his own" (*New Jerusalem and Its Heavenly Doctrine* 22).

Swedenborg is, therefore, concerned with two things: on the one hand, with the development of inner sensory and visionary faculties as the source of true perception, which humanity lost after the "Fall" through outwardly acquired knowledge (our "own"); on the other, with the capacity to distinguish between the truth content of knowledge acquired through outer necessity—because this "knowledge" only serves humans "as a means" "to get smart" (*Heaven and Hell* 356)—and "inner knowledge." This naturally applies to all realms of life and not only for so-called science that seeks to describe the world to men.

Swedenborg never loses touch with reality in which people actually live. But he opposes the outer world's sole determination to give us solutions for life, be they offered as an educational prospectus or a market-oriented choice of career. He attacked the pure rationalism of the Enlightenment, which attempted to dominate the world through human reason and denied the validity of inner knowledge, true illumination, and real enlightenment. He constantly rails against the "reasoners" and "provers," who prefer one-sided rational thought, against the "scholars" who only speculate if something is or not, but seldom assert that it is so. These thinkers have no deeper faculty of conviction connected with the senses of the body" (*True Christian Religion* 333). They have no "inner thinking" that defines the real person; instead, they have succumbed to outward consciousness, to their reason and to learned knowledge, a condition Swedenborg regards as untenable. If intellect dominates, without inner participation and consideration of his or her own life-love or "will," a person is merely "external" and a "hollow image" (*Divine Providence* 311). "Everything that is proved by the will and by reason remains eternally, but not that proved by reason alone, because that which is only a matter of reason is not in man" (*Divine Providence* 319).

Such knowledge finds no echo in his inner world or soul and, therefore, represents no real truth for the individual, a truth that is experienced and lived through the soul. From an evolutionary point of view, such a person is still on a lower level because whoever simply "uses his reason, without a deeper grasp of truth, things are still cloudy for him" (*Heaven and Hell* 271).

Once people have actually recognized the truth for themselves, then they no longer need to explain with their intellect, because they simply know "that it is so" (*Heaven and Hell* 270). They need no persuasion or proof; indeed, they do not even bother with the concept of faith. They have found the truth in themselves, and this is for Swedenborg the perfection of life, not in thought, "but in the remembrance of the truth from the light of truth" (*True Christian Religion* 42).

Everyone should learn to rely to the best of his or her knowledge and conscience on this irresistible inner certainty that stirs in listening, interpreting, and working on information and even one's own thoughts, for they tell one on all levels of conscience what is true or false: "As soon as certain people hear the truth, they remember in an instant that it is true . . . and there are others who do not remember the truth but have to derive it from the proofs of outer phenomena" (*True Christian Religion* 42). The various steps of conscience and the successive states of soul are the sextant of inner development and the purity of intentions. "The real spiritual life of a person is in having a true conscience. Faith is conjoined to love. A person has internal happiness and peace when acting according to conscience, and is in pain when acting against it. This pain is called the pangs of conscience" (*New Jerusalem and Its Heavenly Doctrine* 133).

The fear of drifting off into subjective fantasies leads many people to an ascetic reductionism of materially proven facts. Swedenborg places great value on a highly developed inner discrimination between outer knowledge and one's own discovery of truth. Truth or harmony perceived in the outer world or a theory tells us what is true and valid for ourselves, because we are "the sensorium of the world," "the creature who sits like a spider at the center of his web, the center of perception in which all movements and events of the universe are reflected unchanged."[1] This is the meaning in the teachings of esoteric literature and Eastern philosophy that all knowledge is within ourselves. Once we encounter outer information, which accords with us in feeling and reason, we have a feeling of recognition and knowledge, which is equivalent to both intuition and remembrance, but it is only true for that single person. Thus, Swedenborg says, "If he thinks about something, reads or hears about something, he sees in his inner world whether it is true or not" (*True Christian Religion* 361). But only if he can see into his inner world. Only if this truth accords with our disposition is our attention drawn to it, is it recognized by a "deeper remembrance," "for thinking springs from disposition, and so arises that recognition which is characterized as faith (*True Christian Religion* 231). This faith is the perception or the "exchange" that occurs in the "bank" (*True Christian Religion* 11) of consciousness, which gives us firm conviction and a sure feeling of being on the right path. Then inner and outer form, heaven and earth, are in tune, as we read in the famous Chinese *Book of Changes*, the *I Ching*.[2]

True intelligence and wisdom consist in seeing and grasping what is true and good from what is false and evil, and clearly distinguishing between them, on the basis of a deeper insight and perceptiveness. There are inner and outer things in everyone: the former belong to the inner or spiritual man, the latter to the outer or natural man. When the inner levels have been formed in heaven, then whatever occurs there flows into the outer levels that are derived from this world and forms them to be responsive—that is, to act as one with the inner levels. Once this occurs, "man sees and experiences from the inner world out" (*Heaven and Hell* 351).[3]

If people really act from the inner world outwards and their actions and thoughts are both in harmony, they will feel conviction in the rightness of their action. Of course, the legitimacy of conviction is a very difficult matter to judge. Even the fool, and above all the fanatic, is often "deeply convinced" of the rightness of his or her thoughts and actions. Aren't we all only on the path to ultimate truth? All the greatest thinkers have conceded, "I know that I know nothing." Nevertheless, we may indeed think, speak, and act from "inner conviction," however temporary our perception may be. Whenever we act against our inner conviction, we are responsible for the consequences because "whenever reason does not accord with the will, emotion is torn in twain. That is the case with those who profess a belief but live otherwise" (*Arcana Coelestia* 35).

The usual consequence is inner conflict and discord, accompanied by mental turmoil, ordeal, and desperation. They provoke, mostly in mid-life, a conversion and a so-called "spiritual rebirth," to use Swedenborg's terminology. The path of conversion leads from without to within. It is the path of salvation that all people must walk in order to be "reborn." "It is namely a heavenly mystery," says Swedenborg, "that man is directed and led by the Lord through his own, his deceived senses and his appetites to the true and the good" (*Arcana Coelestia* 24). The self-deception and apparent mistakes are stages of becoming more conscious, the path of "preparation" (*Arcana Coelestia* 29), which leads us to our true self, if we so will.

According to Swedenborg, we are still in the initial stages on the path of "preparation." The first stage of development may end in early youth or even very late in life, because it embraces "childhood as well as the state immediately prior to rebirth" (*Arcana Coelestia* 7).

Swedenborg states that the actual developmental process of the soul unfolds usually in the second half of life, thus in adulthood, like the process of individuation in the psychology of C. G. Jung. At this stage, the capacity to apprehend by empirical means, that is through one's own experience, has been well developed. By this time, a person is "his own master and dependent on his own will and reason" (*True Christian Religion* 106), "which does not occur until a mature age" (*Arcana Coelestia* 3518), when he is self-determining and independent. At this point, an individual often falls into a deep life crisis in which all previous convictions and values are tested and he wonders about the real meaning of life.

For Swedenborg, this situation corresponds to the second day of creation in the Bible or the "second state," which "seldom" occurs "without temptations, misfortune and sorrow quietening and deadening the carnal and mundane impulses of the human ego [own]. In this way the outer world of man is separated from what belongs to the inner world and the inner world contains the remnants that the Lord has kept hidden up until this moment for this purpose" (*Arcana Coelestia* 8).

Here begins the true path of self-knowledge, which is simultaneously divine knowledge and knowledge of the inner self, for "the Self is Brahman," as the Upanishad says. The self is God, whose vessel is the human being, according to Swedenborg.

Before the process of "rebirth," before transformation and new thought can begin, we do not yet know anything of our immanent divinity (*Arcana Coelestia* 17) and our spiritual form, which is the soul. Yes, we don't even know "that there is an inner man, let alone how he is constituted" (*Arcana Coelestia* 6).

According to Swedenborg, the inner world of the human being consists of "three essential elements," "namely, the soul or the heart, the will and the reason. These three are the vessels of those three general principles; the soul itself, or the heart, is the vessel of the Lord for it lives by him; the will is the vessel of love or goodness; and the reason is the vessel of wisdom or truth" (*True Christian Religion* 712). "The faculty from which reason comes takes its entire contents from the influx of wisdom from God. If man doesn't have the right wisdom and the right love, this capacity does not develop, but closes up and so long as they are closed the reason just remains mere reason and the will mere will, but in their essence they are not that" (*Divine Love and Wisdom* 30).

That means that only the outer acquired wisdom is taken for real knowledge, while the genuine wisdom comes from within and manifests in consciousness as the real "truth" and intuitive knowledge. This is equivalent to the concordance of a truth, which encounters our inner world and innermost disposition from outside. After the loss of "paradise," that which comes from outside must stand up to comparison and the test of conscience through our inner capacity to judge. But if it coincides with our innermost "love," our inner desire, it will be recognized by an inner faith and perceived as true, provided that the significance of the inner event is recognized or even guessed. "Outer men," on the other hand, "hardly know anything besides faith in science, which they describe as insight and wisdom; for they don't even know what love is, and mostly they don't even have the right concept of will and reason, and that both form a *single* heart" (*Arcana Coelestia* 113).

Outer men or women prefer not to rely on their inner knowledge or even deny it, conduct that can eventually lead to severe mental problems. If the gulf between feeling and thinking, wanting and being, or the inner and outer situation in reality becomes too wide, neurosis, depression, or psychosomatic disorders usually result. Inner conflict and feelings of emptiness and meaninglessness induce a questioning of all values and lifestyle. If, by his own efforts or the help of others, an affected man achieves an insight that he must change himself from within, the process of change and renewal begins, which was always present as such, but unrecognized, ignored, or even suppressed.

The conversion is foremost a decision of the heart—for the heart corresponds to the will (*Arcana Coelestia* 105, *Divine Love and Wisdom* 398)—but it must be made consciously as an existential decision. It is an inner desire, which manifests clearly in consciousness and must be accepted with complete clarity and resolution.

Once the heart is ready for this change, one is attentive to all helpful insights, be they in the form of therapeutic support or through books, teachers, or friends who accompany the path of conversion and contribute the necessary insight for the inner soul work. People living in the Western world can benefit especially from such "acquired" knowledge, because the conversion, the path of renewal—in Swedenborg's terms the path of rebirth and becoming a fully realized human being—proceeds "from the outer to the inner man" (*Arcana Coelestia* 64), and often moves from painful experiences in the outer world to inner withdrawal. From this voluntary "involution" springs true "evolution."[4] Only on this inner path, according to Swedenborg, can we increasingly resemble the image of God, because God is in each person "and his life from the innermost out" (*Divine Love and Wisdom* 359). According to Swedenborg "God is the real man, out of which every man is a man, depending on his uptake of love and wisdom" (*Divine Love and Wisdom* 289).

A human being is a vessel of the Divine, which assumes a unique spiritual and human form in every one of us, according to each person's duty, constitution, and inner preparation. Thus, a woman becomes, according to her discovery of the inner world, ever more the image of the cosmos or "heaven"—as Swedenborg says—a microcosm in the macrocosm. "For heaven is in man, wherever he may find himself" (*Arcana Coelestia* 3884). This also means, that the woman is always at the center of the universe and that all knowledge is always in her. She must only find access to it.

Before a person can really change, he or she must convert and "atone." In this context, atonement is not the same as repentance and recantation, but signifies the vision or inner purification required for a fundamental transformation. That is why the Greek word for atonement (*metanoia*) means "raising of one's consciousness beyond its normal dimensions. It is the change of the inner man . . . a spiritual rebirth."[5] The "state" of "atonement," following the path of "preparation" and the profound life crisis, is the third step or the third day of creation on the path of human progress (*Arcana Coelestia* 9). It concerns the examination of one's own desires and their occult motivation and intention. "The will is therefore the actual house, in which man dwells, while reason is but the porch through which he comes and goes" (*True Christian Religion* 533). The decision to convert must come from within and be consciously willed; otherwise, transformation is impossible: "rebirth is first and foremost related to the will and only secondarily to the reason. Reason in man resembles light in the world, but the will represents its warmth. As is well known, life and growth can only be fostered by light when warmth is present" (*True Christian Religion* 602). It is patently clear that Swedenborg is talking of an honest "self-examination," because "atonement without self-examination" (*True Christian Religion* 530) is impossible if the development of human virtues and the exercise of true neighborly love in all walks of life is to proceed. We are talking about overcoming the love of oneself and the world and replacing them with selflessness, the love of God, the responsibility and work for the common weal. This is the basis of Swedenborg's spiritual and ethical concept, valid for the whole of humankind.

What are the causes of misconduct or insurmountable problems in one's personal life? Spiritual inertia or hectic activity preventing one from dealing with problems must be overcome in order to induce a change of direction and lifestyle. The precondition in classical esoteric literature is always a new view of things and a different attitude. That all sounds very simple; but, in practice, the greatest obstacle is giving up well-worn, comfortable patterns of behavior and thought. Swedenborg characterizes these inner struggles as "pangs of conscience":

> A struggle then begins, because the inner man is educated by truths and sees what is evil and false in his outer or natural person . . . which proceed from both types of will. (*True Christian Religion* 596)

In the process of education reason plays the foremost and will the secondary role, but the situation is reversed in the state of regeneration. The will takes the chief part, and the understanding the second; nevertheless, the understanding now acts from the will, and not the will through the understanding. (*True Christian Religion* 105)

After "education," the real "transformation" or "rebirth" begins, whenever a "spiritual being" should arise from a "natural man." "As soon as this state arises and begins to complete itself, a fundamental change in emotion occurs. Thought and feelings are in agreement; a person speaks from faith and acts from love—a spiritual renewal takes place" (*True Christian Religion* 571).

Not until the fourth stage does the discovery of the inner world, inner vision, become detectable and the Divine start to stream in to conscious thought. The man or woman now becomes more and more aware that life and truth come from within and begins to see that she lives and acts not through herself but through God and that everything that she considers her "own" is dead in itself (*Arcana Coelestia* 39-41). For this "own," or the ego we falsely consider the true "self," is, according to Swedenborg, "an impure and extremely dirty source," for the person constantly thinks of "gain and self-justification" (*Arcana Coelestia* 874). The goal is to achieve self-lessness that culminates in overcoming the lower ego. In the course of this soul work, a person becomes increasingly aware of insights from within and so receives the true "light" that penetrates his or her consciousness. "[He] is seized by love and illuminated by faith" (*Arcana Coelestia* 9).

Nevertheless, all people remain subject to constant wavering of thought and feeling during this rebirth on the path to becoming a "spiritual" and "heavenly" person. "States of lifelessness and true life" (*Arcana Coelestia* 933) alternate, "principally due to the ascent into the inner world and renewed lapses into the outer world" (*Arcana Coelestia* 10, 134). There is a continual "struggle" between "good" and "evil." The reason for this is that the person prior to rebirth "is completely dominated by his appetites" (*Arcana Coelestia* 59).

The goal of this soul work and spiritual growth is the complete surrender of the personal or outer will. One's own will and thought should be utterly subordinated to the will of God, who works in each person, in order that the true divine consciousness can unfold from within.

At the fifth stage, the person finally expresses him- or herself

> by faith grounded in reason, which strengthens him in truth and goodness. Whatever proceeds from him is ensouled and is known as "fish of the sea" and "birds of the air."
>
> The utterances and deeds of man at the sixth stage of rebirth proceed from this faith, but then they proceed from love grounded in the will . . . and because he now begins to act in faith and love together, he becomes a spiritual man, known as 'image.'" (*Arcana Coelestia* 48)

But even at the sixth stage, the inner world of the spiritual human being is still assailed from the outer world. "The outer world does not wish to follow and serve the inner world and thus struggle still prevails" (*Arcana Coelestia* 91), "and yet the person remains victorious. Inner ties determine his action: the bands of conscience" (*Arcana Coelestia* 81).

There is a very decisive difference between the spiritual person at the sixth stage and the heavenly one on the seventh stage. The spiritual person is only the "image" of God; he or she is "not similar but created likewise. But the heavenly person *is* 'similar' or 'identical' to God." (*Arcana Coelestia* 51).

The heavenly person corresponds to the seventh day of creation. The work of God was completed, and he rested from his work, because all inner struggles in the spiritually most developed individual had ceased. The "spiritual rebirth" is completed: the outer world "follows and serves" the inner world, "the struggle ceases and rest begins" (*Arcana Coelestia* 91):

> Whenever evil and falsehood assault him, he does not care, and

thus he is called victorious. He is free and no longer determined by visible ties. The insights of good and truth, which he has internalized are his invisible bands. (*Arcana Coelestia* 81)

The heavenly man does not act according to his own desires but according to the pleasure of the Lord, which has become his only desire. Therefore he enjoys inner peace and contentment. (*Arcana Coelestia* 85)

[Cosmic consciousness streams from within into conscious thought.] Everything is ordered as in heaven and indeed by dint of its influence in a man who is truly reborn. (*Arcana Coelestia* 2556)

In *Arcana Coelestia* 87, we are told that, because the moment in which the inner struggles of man cease and he becomes heavenly, this day is called Sabbath or the day of Peace." The seventh day is, therefore, "the union of the Divine Self with the humanity of the Lord" (*Arcana Coelestia* 10), the true salvation of humanity from our ties with the material world and our becoming one with the Creator.

The spiritual rebirth is the rebirth of the spiritual person who is ensouled by heavenly peace, which Swedenborg also describes in his biblical exegesis and the inner sense common to all great religions and hidden in their holy scriptures.[6] The birth of the spiritual person is the esoteric meaning of all religions. It corresponds to the inner sense of the Koran, the holy text of Islam. Islam means "peace," just as the inner sense of the Jewish greeting *shalom* and yoga of Eastern religion mean "peace":

Divine peace is in the Lord and arises from the union of the Divine itself and the divine-human in it. . . . For this reason one used to greet each other in the ancient world with words still used today: "peace be with you!" In remembrance of these things the Sabbath was instituted and named after rest or peace. (*Heaven and Hell* 286-287)

As I have experienced this peace . . . I can also describe it, certainly not literally as it is in itself—for human words are not adequate— but by comparison with the peace of mind of those who are content in God. (*Heaven and Hell* 284)

The end of the "holy war, the struggle within," the "defeat of one's own imperfection" brings about this peace.[7]

Swedenborg's exegesis of the creation story in the Old Testament can be compared with the development of consciousness and apprehension of God in the religious texts of the East. Becoming a human being means becoming similar to God—his image—and unfolding the Divine in the human. This supreme goal is a gift of mercy, which humans can only attain through "divine grace" according to Swedenborg. Only thus can the senses' deception and materialist thinking be overcome and absolute truth behind phenomena be glimpsed through an inner conversion.

In the East, the seeker is initiated through spiritual training into the high art of meditation. Only thereby is true self-knowledge and union with God possible. The religious writings of the East give precise guidelines. In the Upanishads, we read:

Bring the stream of feelings and thoughts under your control in order that the supreme reality, the illuminated Lord, manifests himself to you. Strive solely for eternal bliss.

Use your reason and judgement to keep your senses from adhering to the things of pleasure. They will then be purified by the light of divine purity within and this light will manifest itself to you. Be master of your breath and inner powers, light the Self in you through meditation, get drunk on the wine of Divine love . . . so will you attain perfection.[8]

Swedenborg applied himself to various breathing and yoga exercises without any conscious knowledge of the Eastern practice of meditation. These exercises led to heightened states of consciousness, facilitating his spiritual vision. In his so-called spiritual diary, he actually once mentions that he had learned several breathing exercises from Indian spirits, "in order that I might know these things from direct experience" (*Spiritual Diary* 402). In another reference, he expressly indicates that the "men of the early church . . . had perceived different states of love and faith by means of different types of breathing, which changed in the course of time among their successors" (*Arcana Coelestia* 97).

Swedenborg considered that the secret of breathing was completely unknown to men of his own era, but the "ancients" knew of it. He himself was able to reach the supreme state of *samadhi*, the blissful mystical union of Eastern meditative practice, through his own method of breathing. He writes, "My spirit seemed to fly up . . . and descended in an inconceivable circular movement whose center was love" (*Journal of Dreams* 26).[9] Whoever attains the high stage of self-development on this path, raising him- or herself above the senses, has attained the supreme goal of humankind. This recalls a verse in the *Bhagavad Gita* (vi, 8):

> He is a Yogi, a Perfect One;
> Wise, his heart is full of happiness;
> Illuminated, his soul is set on high,
> He is master of his senses.[10]

And parallel to Swedenborg's description of the "heavenly person" whose state only few "of those who are reborn" attain (*Arcana Coelestia* 13), only that person who has reached Swedenborg's state of consciousness corresponding to the seventh day of creation in Genesis attains true wisdom according to the *Bhagavad Gita* (xiv, 22–25):

> [Krishna says]
> Whoever can, without losing equanimity,
> Stand the glare, the fire of desire,
> The dark night of madness,
> When they are near

Nor feel bitterness through want;
Whoever is unperturbed,
Contemplating the play of nature
Says: "It is the law!"

Whoever, takes neither pleasure nor pain,
To whom a stone, a lump of gold, friend and foe
Are all alike, whoever is always peaceful,
Beyond praise and blame;

Whoever no longer desires nor fears
Anything in the world, recognizing
The law which rules over all;
He is a conqueror of nature.[11]

The Bible is the Holy Scripture of the West, but Swedenborg claims that it is encoded in symbolic language as a book of revelation. Thus, it can never be understood literally but only through a new revelation. It is, therefore, decisive for Swedenborg that God "opened the face of His spirit" to him (*True Christian Religion* 779) and reclaimed his inner world in this fashion, from which the true knowledge streamed into his consciousness, and which he passes on to humankind through his writings. Through his scientific work, Swedenborg had a highly trained and disciplined intellect to grasp and describe the sense of this revelation. His financial means allowed him to have his writings printed at his own expense.

Swedenborg had to climb the steps of rebirth through his own transformation, until he reached the stage in which he realized his own inner self. His own ascent and rebirth consisted in "representing the inner man which is opposed to the other."[12] Only thus could he envision the unity of the spirit, the constitution and all-embracing whole of the universe and the connection of humanity with God through our soul in full consciousness with undimmed senses, as they are described through the inner sense of the Bible.

Swedenborg refers exclusively to the Bible. He refers again and again to the "ancients" and "wise," "who were called Sophi," who also possessed true knowledge of the unity and constitution of the universe, from which humanity had come adrift, in his opinion—especially in his own era, the European Enlightenment. "But those old Sophi lived before the times of the Scriptures so that we no longer have any insight into their ancient wisdom any more" (*Conjugial Love* 73).[13]

The Bible is not the only and oldest book of truth, although it does contain the whole truth, according to Swedenborg. Swedenborg expounds the Bible for the Christian West, because "religion proceeds solely from Holy Scripture among the Christians (*Conjugial Love* 115). The deepest mystery, the true knowledge, "sanctuary," "light," "Word," or the "Lord" is older than the Bible.[14] The Word "was given to the inhabitants of Asia before the Israelite word, whose historical books are called the wars of Jehova and whose prophetic books are his mottoes; both are named by Moses, Numbers 21, 14, 15 and 27-30" (*Conjugial Love* 77).

In common with other religious texts, the Bible contains "holiness" and is the Word of God. Swedenborg explains the meaning of the "Word" at length, in order to clarify any ambiguity because the "Word" can also mean the Bible:

> The Word is the means of connection, because it is from the Lord and therefore is the Lord. The Word is the link of the Lord to man and of man to the Lord because the divine Truth in its essence is united with the divine goodness and the divine goodness is united with the divine truth. (*Conjugial Love* 128)

Another scholar has noted the importance of the "Word" or "holy syllable" (for example, *AUM*) in both Hindu and Christian religion.[15] Swedenborg says the same: "The Word . . . is the truly essential out of which and through which everything exists" (*Arcana Coelestia* 76–78). Swedenborg expounds the inner or spiritual sense of the "Word," claiming that the East knew about this much earlier than the West. *Ex oriente lux!* Light comes from the East! Thus, we read in Genesis 2:8, "Yahweh, God planted a garden in Eden which is in the East, and there he put the man he had fashioned."

"The Lord is the East" (*Conjugial Love* 261; cf. *Arcana Coelestia* 107–109) is Swedenborg's succinct summary. Men who lived in the "golden age," beyond the threshold "in the East" of "heaven," are in a "state of grace" according to Swedenborg (*Conjugial Love* 77). As "men of ancient days" or the "early church," they were living still in unity with God, in that blissful state of consciousness that subsequent generations lost across the centuries.

It is evidence of Swedenborg's breadth of spirit that it was not only scholars from the whole Western world who were keen to engage with his thought. His significance appears to have been better understood in many respects in the East. D. T. Suzuki, the great interpreter of Zen Buddhism, who translated four works of Swedenborg's into Japanese, tells all seekers in the West: "This is the Buddha for you Westerners—you should read him and follow him."[16] The time is now ripe for this message.

We "Westerners" have a highly developed rational or outer consciousness, but our "inner vision" is still considerably underdeveloped, even though there is a great deal of talk about intuition and creativity nowadays. But the creative ground of being is seldom understood by this. Generally speaking, humanity considers itself the source of inspiration, although we can neither think nor act of our own accord. The influx of the spirit within occurs without our own agency. Swedenborg himself explains how the apparently "own" flows into us: "For several years I have been granted the experience of how the own of man behaves. . . . He believed correspondingly in the truth" (*Arcana Coelestia* 150). Whatever a man becomes aware of and whatever he recognizes is what God works in him and it is not his own "cleverness," for which he considers his thoughts. "Isn't the inner world there for the sake of the outer world, so that it can flow out into it and rest upon it and so manifest—just as a pillar rests on its pedestal. You can see," says Swedenborg, "that the outer world dissolves and bursts like a bubble . . . in which he is one with God in his thinking and desires" (*True Christian Religion* 462).

But most people do not have this kind of consciousness; thus, they lack the one essential insight: "In truth you are always united with the Lord. But you must *know* it. Nothing else is worth knowing" the Upanishads say in tandem with Swedenborg.[17]

We should become aware of our divine nature and destiny in the world, but we may not consider ourselves to be God, a presumption Swedenborg knew all too well and prophesied in the future. His warning is, therefore, as clear as it is drastic:

> May everyone beware that he does not fall into that deplorable heresy that God has poured himself into men and is in them and no longer in himself, while God is everywhere, both within men as well as without them. For He is . . . in all space without space . . . : a heresy which is so repulsive that it stinks like a corpse in the spiritual world. (*Divine Love and Wisdom* 130)

In another reference he says it succinctly: "What comes from God is not God himself, but divine" (*True Christian Religion* 25).

God is absolute consciousness, the "order" (Greek *kosmos*) or "heaven," which reflects itself in humankind's inner world as the microcosm in the macrocosm (*Arcana Coelestia* 6057). The more a man surrenders to God and unfolds this "heaven" in himself, the nearer the human comes to God and the more he becomes a man, because he has a greater share in the cosmic consciousness or the all-embracing whole. Humankind is a "dwelling place" of God in Swedenborg (*True Christian Religion* 697 j); therefore, he describes the human being always as the "church" or "vessel" of God whose perfection corresponds to the degree of his or her spiritual development or share in cosmic consciousness. Therefore, Swedenborg says expressly: "In the inner sense of the word everything that is said of the church in general is valid for each individual of the church, because he couldn't be a part of it if he didn't form a church" (*Arcana Coelestia* 82), or a microcosm in the macrocosm, which carries the knowledge of the whole in itself, which is revealed through the step-by-step discovery of the inner world. "Every man is born with the capacity to see the truths unto the innermost degree" (*Divine Love and Wisdom* 258). It is the individual's personal decision whether he or she is ready to walk the path within or not. All people are equal in having the capacity and the free will to discover their inner world. But rebirth occurs in each person in a particular way. "The difference is just as varied as the faces and attitudes and everyone can be reborn and blessed according to their state. . . . No man lacks these gifts" (*True Christian Religion* 580).

Spiritual rebirth in the Swedenborgian sense does not mean that everyone must become a visionary or a mystic to save his or her soul. Pure vision is given by God as a gift of grace only to a few in this present epoch of human development, but a path of active neighborly love is possible and prophesied for all people, allowing them to proceed from stage to stage in their inner development. According to Swedenborg, the "own" of men is evil itself. Therefore man in himself is nothing but evil and falsehood" (*Arcana Coelestia* 154); but this doesn't mean that we cannot attain salvation and walk the path of inner transformation. On the contrary! The longing for truth and goodness and through it the possibility and necessity of conversion are deeper and more essential than any appetite. Whenever our intentions and the resultant desire and actions are pure and selfless, we can become a "spiritual" person in this way, whose inner bonds are conscience dictating our behavior. There is in Swedenborg an absolutely essential sentence that is valid for every single person and shows the path of eternal grace: "Active love and innocence do not only excuse the 'own' evil and falsehood of man but wipe it away" (*Arcana Coelestia* 164)!

In the selfless unfolding of love and disposition towards the benefit of the whole within humankind is also the opportunity for true self-realization, which can be experienced and lived ever more consciously through the cosmic dawning of the New Age.

Swedenborg, the "visionary of the New Age," which is astrologically characterized as the "Age of Aquarius," was born himself under the sign of the water carrier. According to him, one could describe the Age of Aquarius as a dialogue between the "inner" and the "outer" person. For Swedenborg, "water" symbolized the insights of the "inner man," the truth (*Arcana Coelestia* 24, 25), which is gradually discovered by us through our spiritual evolution in the course of life. Swedenborg was granted spiritual vision in his search for truth by the grace of God. Aquarius is the "water carrier," the human "truth-seeker," who "pours out the Gospel of his discovery for the benefit of mankind at the end of his own quest."[18] One can see in Swedenborg an ideal representative of his own star sign, whose inner meaning he recorded in his work.

Chapter 5

The New Age

When Swedenborg proclaimed the New Age, he called it the "New Church," in which "the outer world was not separated from the inner world" (*Apocalypse Revealed* 918). He made it clear repeatedly that he did not mean a historical confession by the "New Church."[1] Swedenborg's New Church is a "Church of the Lord. It embraces all humankind. Every dweller on earth can become a member of the New Church as soon as he or she longs to recognize God within and thereby gain access to the spiritual world: "For the Church on earth and the heaven of angels work together the way our own inner and outer, spiritual and natural natures do. . . . God created us as dwellers in both worlds" (*True Christian Religion* 14).

This knowledge that we are linked through our inner world to God and the spiritual world and directed by them enrolls us in this New Church, which "recognizes a single God. The divine love of God in the creation of the world aims at nothing other than binding man to himself and himself with man, in order to dwell with man" (*True Christian Religion* 786).

The transformed consciousness, insight, and guidance comes from within and shows the only right direction and leads to perfection. Swedenborg wants to make us aware of this inner alliance with God and to live in this self-consciousness, which is always God-consciousness. We should entrust ourselves to God unconditionally. This is what Swedenborg means by faith in God, which he repeatedly affirms: "Whoever has excluded themselves from the Church and thereby from heaven by denying God, he has closed the inner man in himself in respect of his will and its associ-ated darling disposition" (*True Christian Religion* 14).

There can scarcely be a more positive and life-affirming summons to inner contemplation and conversion, which permits the actual unfolding of consciousness. It is an exhortation to all seeking people, who have sought their salvation without. It is the duty of each person to follow it. But the achievement of this fundamental insight appears to be the greatest stumbling block. Swedenborg writes again and again: "Heaven is in man and whoever carries heaven in themselves, whoever recognize the divine and allows themselves to be led by it enters heaven. Once this lodges in the mind of man, he is led by the Lord" (*Heaven and Hell* 319).

How much misery and futile suffering could be avoided if we heard such words in our earliest childhood! Swedenborg was well aware that such a truth cannot prevail immediately. As a child of his enlightened age, he certainly hoped that his books would produce an effect through the power of education at universities. He there-fore sent them to all universities in Sweden and overseas, to church leaders and professors of known standing. The latter politely expressed their gratitude; but whether they read the books or even took them seriously is questionable. Swedenborg remained ever optimistic, with a proper dose of realism, knowing that the truth would prevail in the course of humankind's evolution. He wrote in one letter: "At present, I am often asked regarding the New Church, when it will commence, to which I reply: 'by and by.' . . . It's known that the Christian church did not gain ground immediately after the Ascension of Christ, but grew gradually."[2] The formation of the New Church is a cosmic evolutionary process, which not only proceeds through the rise of new modes of thought and behavior from generation to generation in their endless variety, but is inherited through the spiritual evolution of humankind. Each individual is affected and even forms the future unconsciously through his or her thinking and inner development. Swedenborg says categorically: "But sinfulness, once rooted in a susceptibility to the same, is inherited by forthcoming generations and can only be purged by rebirth" (*True Christian Religion* 756).

The level of consciousness is also decisive in a change for good and the better! The more new thinking and consequent behavior is established, the stronger and more stable is the resonance and effect on future generations, to recall Rupert Sheldrake's morphic fields once again.

This theme is more topical than ever today. Through the concrete cosmic rise of the New Age, the meaning of inner guidance and transformation is becoming known and spread ever more widely. One could call the members of the Swedenborgian New Church "the Aquarian conspirators" with reference to Marilyn Ferguson's book *The Aquarian Conspiracy* (1980), for they work in small and large networks scattered across the world in all walks of social and political life. They know that everyone can collaborate in the binding work of neighborly love according to their station and ability and regard themselves as integrated parts of that all-embracing whole, which is ever more closely connected through media, high technology, supersonic airplanes, and the global economy.

The real New Age is neither a public nor a sensational affair. It comes about in a highly private fashion within each individual person as an imperceptible and peaceful revolution, none other than spiritual evolution. The more people are inwardly transformed and the more the general level of consciousness rises from generation to generation, the greater will be its effect in the universe, a process whose end cannot be foreseen as Swedenborg has already indicated:

> "As the new heaven grows, forming the inner world of the church in man, the new Jerusalem—the New Church—descends from this heaven to earth. This cannot occur in an instant but only to the

degree that the falsehood of the former churches is overcome. . . . This however only happens in the fullness of time, by which we understand the end of the church." (*True Christian Religion* 784)

Swedenborg divides human history into various religious eras or "churches," which are not to be understood as historical periods, but rather as the "inner history" of humankind or even as the history of "spiritual rebirth, that is the spiritual evolution of mankind of which the last and fifth church is the 'New Church' proclaimed by him.[3] Swedenborg provides a short survey of the religious eras.

The first church, which we characterize as the oldest, began before the Flood. The second church, which we call the old church, extended over Asia and part of Africa: it found its fulfillment and destruction in idolatry. The third church was the Israelite church: it began with the proclamation of the Ten Commandments on Mount Sinai, continued through the written word of Moses and the prophets, and ended with the desecration of the Word; this culminated in the time when the Lord (Jesus Christ) came into the world. Because he was the Word, they crucified Him. The fourth church is the Christian church founded by the Lord through the evangelists and apostles. (*True Christian Religion* 760)

Elsewhere Swedenborg speaks of the "Four Ages" (*True Christian Religion* 762) or the Golden, Silver, Bronze, and Iron Ages and the inner link with God: that love [i.e., marriage love] was like gold in the first age, like silver in the second, like bronze in the third, and like iron in the fourth; and ultimately, it perished. . . . But I am sustained by a hope that this love will be revived by . . . the Lord, because it can be revived"(*Conjugial Love* 78e).

Because the Church—the institutional and the inner—represented "night" (*True Christian Religion* 764) in his era, Swedenborg saw his mission as the proclamation of the New Church. This fifth and last church, according to the inner sense of the Bible, is valid for all times, even those prior to the Bible's composition. This "New

Church" is the New Age, the New Jerusalem, in which all people will once again live in unity with God and so return to the lost paradise.

For Swedenborg, the "essence of the New Church's faith [is] the truth derived from the Word" and the "existence" of the New Church's faith. Thereby, human beings regain their original and lost faculties. These are, according to Swedenborg, "(1) Spiritual sight, (2) Accordance of truths, (3) Conviction, (4) Acknowledgment inscribed on the mind" (*True Christian Religion* 344).

The institutional churches are only necessary as long as we seekers and novices remain imperfect beings. The divine laws of the various world religions are compulsory, as people are still incapable of living without guidance. It is significant that Swedenborg remained to the end of his days a member of the Swedish Lutheran church, even though he criticized it most violently as an institution. The essential point for Swedenborg is that there is only one God in all religions with which everyone can connect if he or she wishes. Therefore, God "saw to it that all people had One Religion and thereby recognized the divine and an inner life. To live in accordance with religion is to live an inner life, as man thereby directs his gaze to the Divine" (*Heaven and Hell* 318).

The individual woman or man must make a new beginning on himself, before any change of personal circumstances or social transformation can manifest. In practice, this is only effective when egoistic and materialistic thinking is given up. That is why Christian neighborly love and the service of the whole are inseparable for Swedenborg from a truly transformed consciousness:

> Anyone who stands in the faith of the Lord and in active love towards his neighbor is a church in particular, while the Church in its universal form is composed of such individuals. (*True Christian Religion* 767)

Thus it is clear, that the Church of the Lord is neither here nor there but everywhere, both within and without the constitutional

church, it's everywhere where people live according to the principles of active love. That's why the Church of the Lord has spread
over the whole globe and yet there is only one Church; for whenever right living rather than doctrine defines the Church, it is
unified. Whenever doctrine defines the Church, you find many.
(*Arcana Coelestia* 8152)

The various forms of doctrine and divine office are like the various senses and entrails in man which contribute to the perfection
of the whole. (*Arcana Coelestia* 1285)

I've heard that the churches which are so many forms of goodness
and truth are as numerous as jewels in the crown of the King.
(*True Christian Religion* 763)

The Church of the Lord has spread all over the earth; it is therefore
universal. All belong to her who have lived according to their religion in the blessedness of neighborly love. (*Heaven and Hell* 328)

Those individuals transformed from within and reborn no longer
need a church in the customary sense, according to the deep meaning of Swedenborgian writings, and the various confessions will melt
to a unity in the spirit. Only thus is Emerson's statement under-
standable, that Swedenborg "with his powerful spiritual personality
[is] actually the last Church Father, whom few can equal."[4]
    More than two hundred years ago, Swedenborg described this
inner metamorphosis of each person, for which more and more
people are now becoming receptive in times of radical change. How
far this inner transformation is really understood in its deepest
significance varies according to the individual. The gradual spiritual
awakening and the inner transformation, which accompanies outer
change, are very subtle and occur in absolute silence. Swedenborg
emphasizes repeatedly that spiritually reborn, transformed people
act, think, and speak from a "new love and insight" (*True Christian
Religion* 105), which comes from within and is given by God. This

makes them members of their "New Church," makes them "trees which bear not only leaves but fruits" (*True Christian Religion* 106). The more this insight grows in people—that inner transformation of the individual is a precondition of a positive change in the whole—the more embracing and effective the New Church will become, and the New Age, the age of awakening consciousness, can proceed with fewer obstacles. We must try to give our existence a personal meaning, in order to fulfill our individual part of the all-embracing whole as well as possible. And that means work and service for the welfare of creation.

Swedenborg sees the duty of humankind both in the world and in a cosmic context. Creation is God's will, even if we can never fully understand its purpose by reason. Swedenborg knows that this sense is evident from its implicit order, in order that we can realize our self in the world as the crown of creation. The purpose of creation is that it has manifested in order that we may traverse the cosmos as a conscious subject, removing the veil of *maya* (illusion) and find our path into the spiritual homeland. The inner evolution of humanity proceeds in tandem with the unfolding of the endless multiplicity of forms in creation. The divine idea manifests itself as heavenly light in the material world of phenomena and within our species.

In this connection, Swedenborg also indirectly answers Rupert Sheldrake's question concerning the origin of morphic fields, namely, the various forms in the universe. As a scientist, Sheldrake gives the hypothetical answer that new patterns are not created at all but only leave their unmanifest state and manifest themselves in the material world.[5] But Swedenborg says quite clearly: "Before the creation God was love and wisdom itself. Both these essences harbored the desire of doing what is useful, for love and wisdom apart from use are mental images. . . . Thus we were created in the image and likeness [of God], that is the form of Divine order, in order to fulfil the purposes of God (*True Christian Religion* 67).

With these words, Swedenborg concludes his own exposition of the world: the universe as a "theater" of the unfolding and realization of the eternal divine potential. It is actualized in the manifestations of utility. Without the universe as a mirror of God, God himself would have no meaning, for meaning arises only when God is recognized by humankind as a vehicle or subject of apprehension. Thus, humanity is the crown of creation, as there is a conscious relation only between us and God, and we are made in God's image. Everything with love and wisdom derives from the primal unity. Everything has an inner and an outer aspect, which derives from these two divine essences, and everything strives to regain this unity and wholeness. As the "purpose" of creation and mirror of the universe, we are vessels of God, who works through us as love and wisdom. Our duty only consists in recognizing God's inherent love and becoming aware of it. Then love and wisdom, inner and outer, harmonize. This explains the sensibility of every individual who wants and ought to make him- or herself useful in the human community. Everyone is equipped with specific hereditary factors and talents, inclinations and gifts, and these can be lived and used to create God-willed utility. Everyone can contribute to the commonwealth by serving the whole in self-realization:

> Love and wisdom apart from good works are not anything; they are merely ideal entities, and they only become real when they exist in use. . . . Apart from wisdom, love is nothing; but in wisdom it takes form for . . . use. (*True Christian Religion* 387 [3])

> One should also know, that the whole man appears in his deeds or works. His wanting and thinking, the love and faith that form his inner world are not complete until expressed in deeds or works. These represent his outer aspect. (*Heaven and Hell* 475)

> Love is the purpose, wisdom the immediate cause, and utility is the effect. This effectiveness is the conclusion, vessel and substance of wisdom and love. . . . Utility is their summation. (*Divine Love and Wisdom* 213)

Swedenborg's work is a unique summons to an active, joyous,

and purposeful life. Everything should and must manifest according to the laws of creation. It must become evident and cannot remain a mere idea, as it has neither sense nor value on its own. According to Swedenborg, every human talent should be actually lived. "But love and wisdom only exist in an ideal manner, namely in the feelings and thoughts of our heart. But in usefulness they exist in reality, namely in the actions and work of the body. . . . Usefulness consists in one following the duties of one's vocation in truth, honesty and zeal" (*True Christian Religion* 744 [3]).

For each individual, the development of human virtues is vital as prescribed in the Ten Commandments and by Jesus Christ in the Gospels. So Swedenborg's biblical exegesis contains the entire doctrine of the New Church or the New Age in which he describes the relationship of the inner and outer human being according to his revealed interpretation of the Bible. The meaning of the world and of humanity is explained therein. Our existence only becomes meaningful when we live according to our inherited factors.

According to Swedenborg, everyone should unfold; moreover, each person is ceaselessly summoned by God to do so. That is the meaning, purpose, and goal of human existence. In agreement with Eastern wisdom teachings, Swedenborg is concerned to persuade people that they must give up "self-love and love of the world"—that is, exclusively egotistical and materialist thinking. For "self-love and love of the world" are hell, falsehood, "while the love of the Lord and the love of one's neighbor prevail in the heavens—yes, they are heaven" (*Heaven and Hell* 554).

Parallel to this, we read in the Upanishads: "Life in the world and life in the spirit are not reconcilable. Work or actions are not opposed to the realization of God; they are even a way to it. Renouncing the world means renouncing the ego and selfishness, but not life" (Isa Upanishad).

It always depends on the right attitude, the transformed consciousness, which regards itself as a part in service of the whole. Then there is no false thinking to obstruct self-realization. That is why Swedenborg says categorically: "But one should note well that the Lord never relegates a man from an honor or the acquisition of wealth, but only from the greed of gaining honors . . . only for the sake of wealth or property" (*Divine Providence* 183).

The banal insight that money alone cannot make one happy often comes at the end of a long struggle for earthly goods and personal power. The platitude that self-love rules the world still seems to do more good than harm. Nevertheless, attitudes change very slowly, and ethics is a meaningless concept for many people. But there are no limits to their benefits when anchored in the right attitude. As an active scientist, member of the Swedish Diet, and a full participant in social and political life, Swedenborg can fill volumes with examples of purposeful action, which is always directed towards the general good. "To create value means: to wish others well for the sake of the general best" (*Heaven and Hell* 64).[6]

Swedenborg never loses sight of reality and the daily life of people. On the contrary, he helps them towards inspired vision and leads them, in a clear-sighted manner, again and again to what is essential, by tirelessly describing all kinds of utility (*usus*). "By utilities are understood not only the necessities of life relating to good, clothing and shelter, but also the good of the country, society and fellow citizens. Every business concerned with the purpose of love is good in this way, when money is loved merely as a serving means and the businessman flees from deceit and evil arts in disgust; but it is different when money is the purpose of love, and business is loved merely as a means; for this is then avarice, the root of all evil" (*Divine Providence* 220).

All this sounds so obvious and well-known, yet it has not really penetrated our consciousness. Things were no different in Swedenborg's time. Swedenborg does not want to change the social order but to work on the thoughts of men and women, by making it clear that they must understand themselves as an integral part of a unified whole, in which they are both givers and takers. Only from this consciousness can a commonwealth truly blossom for the benefit of all. And, in his view, only thus can one truly serve God and not by renouncing worldly things. We must realize our entire heredity in the world to take our place in the next world as an image of our individual inclination. "We can only be formed for heaven through the world. . . . That is the locus of the ultimate effects that give definition to our affections . . . so the practice of charity and growth in its life is possible only to the extent that we participate in the activities in the world but not when we withdraw from them" (*Heaven and Hell* 360).

For Swedenborg, the world and the human community with all its institutions are right the way they are: "No one with healthy reason can condemn temporal goods, for they are like blood in the body of human society. No one can reject the dignities inherent in offices, for they are likewise the hands of the King and the pillars of society—provided, of course, that natural and sensual love is subordinate to spiritual love" (*True Christian Religion* 403 [3]).

But Swedenborg is not talking about a naive and uncritical type of neighborly love piously applied to everyone. On the contrary, it should be practiced with well-considered "cleverness," which presupposes a good knowledge of people. "Whoever loves his neighbor in real charity examines how that person is made and produces good in him according to the nature of his goodness" (*Charity* 15).

Swedenborg is concerned with the proper relations among individuals. Everyone should be a good psychologist and discover how things stand with his or her "inner" person. For we can only really "love" our neighbor if we really feel attracted to our own inner love, which has to be recognized. To allow oneself to be deceived by externals would be mad and stupid, according to Swedenborg. "The good of the inner will is the neighbor, who is to be loved, and not the good of external will, whenever it does not agree with that One" (*Charity* 17). Or, expressed differently: "Everyone is a neighbor according to their spiritual relationship" (*Charity* 18). Only then can an authentic relationship and collaboration occur and harmony develop among people.

No spectacular or revolutionary changes in the world follow Swedenborg's revelations. The advancing spiritual evolution of humanity forms the fifth and New Church. But the inner vision and inner sensibility of people can evolve so far that humanity will find its way back to paradise, lead a life in continual prayer, and outer circumstances will alter accordingly. Men and women of the New Age will "understand and see the divine truths by inner illumination, and live by them" (*Apocalypse Revealed* 920). The "Kingdom of the Lord," "which is the Church" (*Apocalypse Revealed* 596) will come, and all people will live once again in the most heartfelt union with God. "This New Church is the crown of all churches which have existed before on earth, because it will honor a visible God, in which the invisible dwells like the soul in the body. . . . Any union of God with us must also involve our reciprocal union with God, and this reciprocity is only possible with a visible God" (*True Christian Religion* 787).

The New Age will be a religious age in which people are perfectly aware of their alliance with God and the whole universe, and serve the whole in this consciousness. They will be "clairvoyant," "able to see more with *one* glance than our laborious research can ever discover, for the spirit of the coming age will make today's incomprehensible comprehensible. The hostility between spirit and matter which has arisen through our limited consciousness will fade, for the spirit of the New Age will no longer regard matter as alien but they will be able to penetrate and transform it with consciousness. An authentic social conscience is self-evident and the basic needs of life will be provided so that not even the poorest will be forced to earn them laboriously."[7]

On this path, work serves the individual as the service of God, which is done from an inner need and with inner joy. Only then does the effect commence, which alone can make one happy, not wealth and power, but that which brings "inner contentment," climaxing in the conscious awareness that one can realize one's inner desire as a part and for the benefit of the whole. Thus, everyone can find heaven on earth, that inner balance which is "eternal blessedness" for Swedenborg. "This blessedness comes to each by the utility of their office. In every angel's inclination of will there is a hidden vein which drives the heart to some activity and through which it comes to rest and feels content" (*True Christian Religion* 735 [5]).

All of us must, therefore, work to build our own "heaven" on earth by our own exertions and contribute our own personal share to the good of the whole, which is inherent in our particular and individual "love," to fulfil our place in creation. In exchange, we can expect the highest reward after death. One can scarcely find more beautiful or comfortable words to explain the world and human life than these:

> The real purpose of the creation of the universe is nothing but the formation of an angelic heaven out of human beings, where everyone who believes in God may live in eternal happiness. That divine love which is in God and which, essentially is God, cannot intend anything else, and divine wisdom which is in God and is God can produce nothing else. (*True Christian Religion* 773)

The extent to which human beings have realized their "inner" being during their earthly life will become apparent when each enters the "spiritual world," the beyond after death. Here the inner and outer person take their leave. Death is not the end of life, but a transition into the true spiritual life.

Chapter 6

Life after Death

It may come as a surprise to some that there is no ceaseless wheel of rebirth in Swedenborg. The doctrine of reincarnation (literally: becoming flesh again) current today in both the East and West is based on the law of karma. This means that our life is only the consequence of a former life and that, in some way, all our deeds will redound in this or a future life. This idea does not occur in the whole work of the Swedish visionary. Consequently, Swedenborg omits the whole "cycle which transforms the outcome of one life into a new life and destiny,"[1] which must be lived through a new incarnation in this world in order to encourage further spiritual development. In Swedenborg, this occurs in the next world, insofar as it is possible at all. The doctrine of reincarnation is a topic like the idea of life after death on which people differ: neither one nor the other of the two theses has so far been proved scientifically, not even by parapsychology, which has tried so hard to confirm reincarnation through lengthy research projects. The controversial "regression therapies," nowadays so fashionable in America and even in Germany, can provide no sure proof of reincarnation. The famous near-death researchers and doctors such as Elisabeth

Kübler-Ross or Raymond A. Moody, despite contact with many patients in the course of their work, have produced no rigorous scientific results to prove survival after death.[2]

So-called near-death experiences (NDEs) or descriptions of the beyond by people who have been resuscitated following their clinical death are by no means isolated phenomena of our times. They were recorded from Greek antiquity through the so-called visionary literature of the Middle Ages.[3] The belief in these phenomena is common to both thanatology (the study of death) and reincarnation research. Here one simply relies on the statements of those who consciously remember a NDE after his or her return to the body and is capable of describing it—as far as this is possible in our imperfect language, while "regressions" into an earlier life usually occur under hypnosis and are, therefore, subject to the risk of deception and manipulation. For people who have had a so-called "experience of the beyond," their experience is their only proof; they know from their own experience, which can be the only proof for personal knowledge. Everything known on the subject hitherto is, therefore, an anecdotal deposition of subjects who have had such NDEs and out-of-body experiences (OBEs). This means that we are still dependent on ourselves and our beliefs alone, despite all advance scientific research and technical resources. In the last resort, even the reincarnation researchers doubt that reincarnation can ever be proved.[4]

There are just as few proofs for the existence and correctness of Swedenborg's visionary sight into the beyond. His experience and the "revelation of the spirit" are his only proofs for the existence of the world beyond. Here, we are only talking about an inner acceptance of his doctrines, which means an entirely personal belief, in which Swedenborg's writings make sense. The chief subject of his work is always "the inner" person, who is investigated concerning his or her concordance or nonconcordance with the "outer" person in the next world: namely, when the individual's "book of life" is opened, and every single thought and deed is contained. In death, we move from one world to another; therefore, Swedenborg thinks, "that death means resurrection and survival in the inner sense of the divine Word"

(*Heaven and Hell* 432ff). "The spirit of man appears after death in the spiritual world, moreover in human form just as he appeared in the world. He still delights in his capacity to see, hear, talk and feel. . . . We are ourselves in all respects, except that we are not clothed in the gross body we had in the world. This we leave behind and never resume" (*New Jerusalem and Its Heavenly Doctrine* 225).

After his physical death, a man remains in the physical state, "in which he found himself during his life. Thus a man, as soon as he dies, is also ranked in his position" (*Divine Providence* 307). One retains one's entire nature from this world to the next; death is only a transition to the spiritual world, which does not even seem strange, as death is the continuation of life. After death, the man is just as much a man as before and more so" for he knows nothing else besides being in the former world" (*True Christian Religion* 792, 793). There is, however, the distinction that he has a "substantial" body instead of a material one, which is his inner world, his spiritual figure, and which appoints him his place in the next world. Swedenborg does not use the concept of reincarnation but speaks of the "great sages'" belief in "migration of souls," according to which the soul can return to earth and begin a life similar to its former existence and be returned to all its former deeds (*True Christian Religion* 79f; *Heaven and Hell* 256). According to Swedenborg, the soul is an "image of the spirit" and will survive eternally, but it does not return to earth. Every person is a new creation. He sees the significance of humanity rather more in a universal context to whose laws we are subject but about whose order we are instructed through our own inner world, as each person is him- or herself the order of the cosmos. Swedenborg simply considers the "migration of souls" and "speculations" about it "complete nonsense" (*True Christian Religion* 79f).

He speaks rather of a "remembrance of something, that man never saw or heard." This so-called "remembrance," which Swedenborg thought the basis of the "ancients'" belief in the "migration of souls," was recalled by them, "because spirits are influxed from their own memory into the imaginations of their thought (*Heaven and Hell* 256). In such cases, it is not a matter of one's own but alien contents of memory that have possibly encouraged the belief in reincarnation.

This is probably the only point on which Swedenborg does not agree with the wisdom of the "old Sophi and sages," whose doctrines he otherwise quotes concerning life after death (*Divine Providence* 324) and whose wisdom was received by them from God in much the same way as his own "through an influx in their inner world" (*Heaven and Hell* 254).

Rupert Sheldrake's hypothetical reinterpretation of reincarnation is interesting in this context. The idea of "remembrance" falls within his theory of "morphic resonance," treated in chapter 3, "Consciousness," according to which everyone resonates with his or her individual past through personal memory. In the remembering of an earlier life, one could be entering morphic resonance with someone who lived in the past for unknown reasons. "This might help to account for the transfer of memories without our having to suppose that the present person *is* the other person [in the past] whose memories he or she can pick up."[5] Basically, we are talking about the same phenomenon that Swedenborg describes: that a spirit—another morphic field in Sheldrake's terminology—has taken possession of someone's consciousness and thereby caused this deception (*Heaven and Hell* 255). Sheldrake accepts that "the principal way in which we are influenced by morphic resonance from other people may be through a kind of pooled memory," which everyone is subject to if unconsciously, just as people are influenced by the "collective unconscious" described by Carl Gustav Jung.[6]

The unique bodily existence of the human being is a fact for Swedenborg the visionary. The natural scientist Rupert Sheldrake and others can only speculate regarding the belief in reincarnation.

For Swedenborg, it is a human duty to realize our "inner person," that is, our "favorite inclination" as a component of a constantly changing universe in the here and now. According to Swedenborg, all people, of whatever culture, nature, or religion, has the possibility and opportunity to unfold themselves, for only the inner world is the connection to God, whose image we carry within ourselves and which we should realize in the outer world. For inner and outer should ideally correspond already to one another in this world. Thus, a manor woman is examined in the next world, following her death, to establish to what extent her inner and outer worlds match. In the next world, our inner self is made manifest. "In the spiritual world no one may think and desire other than they speak and act. Everyone must be the image of their inclinations" (*Heaven and Hell* 498). Nobody will have a "divided heart," by which Swedenborg means that a person in this world "should recognize nothing besides what he wishes" (*Heaven and Hell* 425) "and should consequently act so as to be happy in his earthly life and blessed in eternity after death. But he will only be happy and blessed if he has acquired wisdom and kept his will obedient" (*True Christian Religion* 588). Only our "inner world," our "love," the real essence of the individual human being, determines our place. "After death the basic inclination or dominant love of each person endures. It is not extinguished in eternity. . . . Thus one can see that man remains in eternity according to his basic inclination or prevailing love" (*Heaven and Hell* 363).

The reason for this is "that man after death can no longer be changed in the same way as he was in the world through instruction. . . . Therefore man remains in eternity as his life and love were in the world" (*Heaven and Hell* 480).

Not until after death will the "degree" or level of consciousness be recognizable, which the person occupied during his or her life. Then he or she enters "the same degree which corresponds to his or her love and wisdom" (*Divine Love and Wisdom* 203):

> Everything that man acquires in this world remains, and he takes it with him after death. It will even be increased and brought to fulfilment, but only as far as within the limits of his affection and desire for what is true and good in it, not beyond. . . . Whoever possesses a great measure will receive more, whoever a smaller, less. (*Heaven and Hell* 349)

The degrees or levels of consciousness are naturally separate from one another. "That's why the angels of the lower heavens cannot ascend to the levels of the upper heavens . . . because the love and wisdom of the latter is at a higher degree beyond the former's apprehension" (*Divine Love and Wisdom* 180).

Just as everything changes and develops in the material world, there is a permanent change among the spirits and angels in the next, which Swedenborg calls "changes of state," independent of time and space yet not dissimilar from mundane states. But he repeats again and again that this change and development can only proceed as far as the degree of inner development permits (*Heaven and Hell* 156), no further. In another passage, Swedenborg writes that every person is given the chance after death to improve his or her life, if possible, by receiving instruction from angels and understanding their truths according to their nature (*Divine Providence* 238), according to their inner state. But man remains within his specific grade of development after death, that is, on his level of consciousness in his own spiritual context and environment. Swedenborg also explains why: "A particular spirit wanted to know what heavenly joy was, so he was allowed to feel it up to the point where he could not hear any more. . . . When we accept what is deepest within us, we are in our heavenly joy. We could not bear anything deeper; it would become painful for us. (*Heaven and Hell* 410).

But within this specific degree of consciousness, limitless evolution is still possible. "Everything can be enriched further and further in eternity, because everything can be made in endless variations, enriched and replicated and made fruitful. Nothing of goodness ever has an end, for it derives from the Eternal" (*Heaven and Hell* 469).

Carl Gustav Jung also reflected much on life after death and the further evolution of consciousness in the next world. He was convinced that the human being can only take the upper limit of knowledge acquired in life into the next world. Jung writes: "That is probably why earthly life is of such great significance, and why it is that what a human being 'brings over' at the time of his death is so important. Only here, in life on earth, where the opposites clash together, can the general level of consciousness be raised. That seems to be man's metaphysical task"[7]

The essential event in the life of all of us is our "spiritual rebirth," which occurs after an existential decision to convert, through which alone a real unfolding of consciousness takes place and enables each person to ascend step-by-step in the course of one's life towards an alliance with the Divine. But this can only happen in our terrestrial life according to divine law, which Swedenborg calls "order."

Swedenborg even has his own use for the law of karma, according to which everyone is judged according to his or her deeds. This "judgment" takes place in the next world, whereby each person is placed in the very "circumstances," for which he or she was responsible. Thus, the life of the human being remains after death as it was in the world: "So we are judged according to our own deeds, not that they are counted up, but that we return to them and behave in the same way. The outmost aspects of our life that we take with us after death become dormant, and [then] act in harmony with our deeper natures." (*Divine Providence* 277).

The idea that a human being accomplishes spiritual development only in this world with the aid of numerous trials in the form of a lesson—which is life itself—accords with the doctrine of reincarnation. In Swedenborg also, true understanding, always identical with the apprehension of God, can only be achieved in the spiritual-physical polarity of earthly life, whenever one is following an inner guide and is steered by "divine providence" in every single thought towards this goal. "Everything spiritual is taken up in the natural world, in order to achieve reality among people. For anything spiritual, in order to be anything with man, must have a recipient in the natural. Pure spirit does flow into us, but we do not accept it. . . . If it is to affect us, there must be perception and then acceptance . . . and this is only possible for us only on our natural level." (*True Christian Religion* 339). "That's why there are no spirits or angels who weren't born as humans" (*Divine Love and Wisdom* 257).

The possibility of the human being's reaching the goal of his or her destiny is concealed in a latent fashion in the soul of each single life and can be used by each person to achieve complete unfolding. In any case, the advocates of reincarnation oppose the theory of a single bodily existence, by saying that it is impossible to achieve perfect understanding and consciousness in a single life. Thus, they think that reincarnation is necessary and will only end once one is completely realized, once the evolutionary process has progressed from slumbering ignorance to total illumination, as one can read for example in the work of the Dane Poul Lauritsen. Lauritsen mentions Swedenborg among many famous European personalities, who "more or less firmly believed in reincarnation."[8] If Lauritsen had really known Swedenborg's works, he would never have committed such a completely unfounded assertion to paper. Nevertheless, he concedes that spiritualism in general does not support the theory of reincarnation, with the major exception of Allan Kardec (1804–1869), the founder of spiritualism in France.

The reason for the persistence of the doctrine of reincarnation may chiefly be the law of karma, which offers the comforting possibility of being able to make restitution for the errors of this life in another, even if the path of the soul should be still full of sufferings or joy. The great Indian Sri Aurobindo, for whom reincarnation is "an existential certainty" opposes the "idea of requital" inherent in the customary, mechanical, and infantile law of karma, which is only a "moral profiteering" to him, having less to do with the meaning of life and a mere a construction "devised by human ignorance."[9] But the common goal of serious advocates of reincarnation is always the evolution of the soul, which is finally supposed to dissolve in immortal consciousness and a full understanding of God. Whether and to what extent this will ever be possible has never been answered at this point.

What is certain is that neither reincarnation nor survival after death could be proved with the usual scientific methods and probably should not be proved. The belief in survival after death is a very private affair for every individual, an inner knowledge that requires no external proof. In this question, all people are reliant upon themselves and their trust in God, which allows them to hope for a continuation of life after death. Here faith is the sole key to understanding and perhaps the precondition for its realization.

The widespread inability of people to believe seems to be the real spur for spiritualism and the channeling wave of the present. People want to douse their fear, a "proof" for survival after death. But the individual, nevertheless, remains dependent on the inner knowledge of his or her soul, which is the sole court of true understanding. It is important that what Swedenborg calls the chance "to recognize God," given to each and every human, be used in this present earthly life, in order to recognize each person's reconnection, his or her religion with God. For "man was created in order to be united with God" (*True Christian Religion* 369). This is the "destiny of humanity," which can only be fulfilled through the conversion of humans to God. It "is the return of the lost son." And this conversion or "turning homeward" always happens by free will. Inge von Wedemeyer writes "man is free to become alienated. And he is also free to convert. At any time!"[10]

This connection with God exists in each man or woman through her inner world, about whose meaning she must become aware as far as possible in order to discover it and allow herself to be led by it by God, according to his nature and order. For this reason, the meaning of the coming of Jesus Christ into the world was so important for Swedenborg, who attacked the literal biblical exegesis of the institutional church in the most violent fashion in his writings, because he shows humans how their connection and union with God occurs through their inner world. God had to become man in order "that the union with God and so salvation might be granted to humans through this incarnation" (*True Christian Religion* 98); this depends alone on the understanding and recognition of God in order to heal him (the English word *whole* expresses this much better).

This interpretation of the meaning of the figure of the savior has nothing to do with literal belief and doesn't even correspond to the opinion of the confessional churches, against whose dogmas Swedenborg wrote for twenty years. But its topicality today can scarcely be greater. Although the incarnation of God as man in Jesus

Christ is the central theme of Swedenborg's work, he does not treat of this any less objectively and clearly than any other problem; he approaches the subject scientifically whenever he explains the reason Jesus had to come into the world and had to accept the frightful death on the cross. In order for the gospel of Jesus to be received by humans, God had to take account of his own order and even accept the human fact, because "every thing must match the other, before a dialogue or reciprocal action is possible between them." (*True Christian Religion* 125). This law is valid for each and every thing in the whole universe, even for God. He could not even act against his own law: "There is a law of order, that God must approach the human, get to know him and unite inwardly with him in the same way that a human can approach God and get to know him" (*True Christian Religion* 89).

God cannot directly approach the human being, as we on account of our nature could not even tolerate such an encounter. He had to send something similar to the human being, the "Son of Man" into the world, in order that the latter could proclaim the truth about God to humans. Therefore, through his incarnation, Jesus made himself "useful to God," "a vessel or a dwelling," which God could enter (*True Christian Religion* 105). God revealed himself as man in Jesus in order to show us that the Divine can only be taken up in this material world by the human being.

But the suffering of Christ was not itself redemption. The church has left humankind in this error right up to the present. Swedenborg consequently rejects all the dogma of centuries and expounds the meaning of Jesus Christ in a completely new fashion—in his doctrine of the inner and outer, as it was proclaimed by Jesus according to Swedenborg. By his death on the cross, Jesus has demonstrated to humanity his unshakable belief and the connection and unity with the Father, with God. His inner conviction, his faith, his knowledge of God, and his connection with the Father through his inner world gave Jesus the spiritual strength to take death upon himself, in order to give humanity a sign. Jesus showed us how we can achieve redemption, by recognizing God within, entrusting ourselves to him, and accepting our appointed destiny. But the death on the cross was not redemption itself for Swedenborg. "Rather the Lord incessantly redeems all those who believe in him and act according to his words" (*True Christian Religion* 579). For Jesus taught "that the inner and the outer man should form a unity. But this means nothing else besides being born anew" (*True Christian Religion* 326); and, according to Swedenborg, this only happens through inner transformation, conversion, or, in Swedenborg's words, through "spiritual rebirth," which resurrects the connection with the divine *urgrund*, which Jesus embodied in a perfect manner:

> For this very reason the Lord came in an orderly fashion into the world in order to make the human Divine, that is to say, he wanted to be born like any other person, and taught like any other, and born again like any other, but with this difference, that man was born anew of the Lord. . . . The regeneration of man is an image of the glorification of the Lord; or what is the same, that in the process of the regeneration of man may be seen as in an image, although remotely, the process of the Lord's glorification. (*Arcana Coelestia* 3138)

According to Swedenborg, God became human through Jesus. Through him, the true light came into the world, in order for it to be recognized by humankind. Jesus brought the truly perfect consciousness, the pure and sacred Christ-consciousness into the world as it is proclaimed above all in the Gospel of John, from which Swedenborg, in *True Christian Religion* 107, repeatedly quotes Jesus' own words as proof regarding spiritual rebirth: "'I have come as light into the world, that whoever believes in me may not remain in darkness" (John 12: 46). "While you have the light, believe in the light, that you may become sons of light" (John 12: 36). But Jesus was, according to Swedenborg, "a child like any other child in his human nature, a boy like any other boy. . . . The only difference was that he went through this evolution, faster, more comprehensively and completely than others" (*True Christian Religion* 89), an evolution which, in

Swedenborg's words, was never equaled before and has not been equaled since. "That's why we read in John: 'No one has ever seen God, apart from the only begotten Son' (John 1: 18), and therefore there is no access to the Father except through him. Thus he is the means" (*Arcana Coelestia* 4211).

This is the deep and innermost meaning underlying Swedenborg's biblical exegesis and the evangel, which he wishes to communicate to us. If the final fulfillment of life should not lie in the next world, in the return to God, the death of Jesus Christ on the cross would be completely pointless; the cross points to redemption after death, whenever our faith and conception of God are revealed through our inner being. When inner and outer accord, then the person is whole; only then is he or she redeemed. For Swedenborg, "Father" and "Son," "Divine and human" are perfectly united in Jesus, like "body and soul" (*True Christian Religion* 98).

For humans, this signifies a challenge, which has been beautifully formulated by Thomas Noack: "But when Christ's work was an inner work, then our work which follows is also an inner work."[11] This is the realization of the inner self, the "ruling love," which Jesus perfectly realized. According to Swedenborg, Jesus reached the highest stage of human evolution "because he glorified the naturally Human to its final perfection; that is why he was resurrected in the body, which does not happen with any other people" (*Divine Love and Wisdom* 221).

This perception of God is always an inner knowledge and equivalent to faith and its resultant insight, but it can only be a matter of an inner process whose effect can manifest in a variety of ways in the outer world. "The Divine is no different from one agent to another, but one agent is created differently from another. This is why the Divine appears different in its representations" (*Divine Love and Wisdom* 54), but it is always the same in essence. This is the basis of the commandment of mutual tolerance and true neighborly love, which plays such a central role in Swedenborg's thought. For him, reincarnation and a new earthly life are completely superfluous for obtaining the knowledge of God, which so-called "simpletons" often possess more than "rationalists." The latter must prove everything by external phenomena, while "simpletons" rely on their inner knowledge, which presumes no intellectual ability, but which contains the truth accessible to everyone, whatever their station in life.

Advocates of reincarnation see its necessity in the explanation the law of karma offers for the apparent social, cultural, and material injustice of the world. It also teaches that each soul brings the sum of all its experiences from prior lives and the continuity of its evolution into every successive life. In Swedenborg, human beings are embedded in the simultaneity of all events in the whole universe, as time and space are only relative and simply apply to materialistic thinking. In the spiritual realm, there is no time and space: "the future is present or what will happen, has happened" (*Arcana Coelestia* 730 [5]). If this simultaneity of all-embracing eventfulness did not obtain, there could be no mutual exchange between everything in the cosmos, as this presupposes simultaneity. At this point, we should remember Swedenborg's words quoted in the first chapter: "This all-embracing whole composed of the smallest parts is such a coherent unified work, that no single point touches and can be excited without the sensation being transferred to all other parts" (*True Christian Religion* 60). Thus, every spiritual stirring of any single existence has an effect on all humans, even if this is not rationally explicable.

Every person, according to Swedenborg, is born with complete knowledge. But the human being does not know it. Still, we have the ability to attain all knowledge that is hidden in us (*True Christian Religion* 48), through the opening of our inner world, which occurs through our second birth, our rebirth. "This inner world is in every person, who is born" (*New Jerusalem and Its Heavenly Doctrine* 224). Swedenborg always means an inner knowledge, which leads to true understanding and recognition of God and which is equally present in every person, even if he or she is born without "foreknowledge." Swedenborg gives us the following explanation as to how we become those much-quoted vessels:

> because we are not life, but the recipients of life, it follows that our
> conception of our father is not the conception of life, but merely the
> conception of the first and purest form receptive of life, to which
> substance and matter are added step by step in the womb of the
> mother, in forms suited to receive life in its order and degree.
> (*Divine Love and Wisdom* 6)

Conception in the womb is accordingly the creative act of the
soul, which can only occur in this world, as the precondition of the
apparent polarity between inner and outer, physical and spiritual,
ideal and material obtains on earth. And as the Divine, substance
and form are everywhere and always the same, it is also ready to
unfold its full form and uniqueness in every human, which is equivalent to true self-knowledge and the fulfilment of the assignment
given to each in his or her appointed station. There is no reference
anywhere in Swedenborg to a rebirth in the body. There is no reincarnation in Swedenborg's exposition of the world. His worldview
is complete without it.

It is a remarkable fact that even the advocates of reincarnation
advance the view that one has no knowledge of one's earlier lives,
as these could hinder present development and free unfolding,
because this knowledge of one's earlier mistakes would only
confirm whatever could be found in the present life. This seems to
have been proved in reincarnation research, as the suspicion arose
that those regressions described as "pre-lives" could have been
projections of fears and wishes dominating the present life.[12]

As a rule, only negative, terrible, and very unfortunate memories are "tapped," which are confirmed by similar experiences in the
present. There are ostensibly no reports of people who remember
under regression beautiful and happy incidents in their previous
lives. Only human suffering seeks such an explanation, ignorant
that the solution must be found in the here and now and within.
Even if reincarnation were true, we would know nothing of it. Sri
Aurobindo also teaches this: "The law that robs us of remembrance
of past lives is a law of cosmic wisdom; it doesn't hinder but serves

the purpose of evolution."[13]

If this is so, then it naturally poses the question whether reincarnation is meaningful or justified at all. Perhaps its advocates cling to it so tightly because they see no possibility of achieving complete happiness or solving their problems in only one life. Everyone probably asks such a question at some stage, even if the person does not necessarily think of reincarnation. The question concerning the meaning of life and survival after death is asked again and again by every human being and must be answered by each one in his or her own way. The solution is hidden within each person. We must only know that we are linked with God through our soul, through our inner world. The moment of its recognition is the beginning of the process of rebirth, which brings the longed-for salvation. Rebirth is of such decisive significance in Swedenborg, for it is through spiritual rebirth that the transformation from the outer to the inner person is accomplished. Thus, we all find our inner support and inner guide, which assists us to live in harmony with ourselves and the Creator.

NOTES

Chapter 1: Life, Work, and Influence

1. Ralph Waldo Emerson, *Representative Men: Seven Lectures* (London: Henry G. Bohn, 1850), 50.

2. Ernst Benz, *Emanuel Swedenborg,* translated by Nicholas Goodrick-Clarke (West Chester, Penna.: Swedenborg Foundation, forthcoming).

3. Seyyed Hossein Nasr, *Knowledge and the Sacred* (New York: Crossroad, 1981), 130–134.

4. Benz, op. cit.

5. As is customary in Swedenborgian studies, the numbers following titles refer to paragraph or section numbers, which are uniform in all editions, rather than to page numbers.

6. Benz, op. cit.

7. Stephen Larsen, *Reisen nach Innen* (Zurich: Swedenborg Verlag, 1986), 23–29.

8. Benz, op. cit.

9. *Die Bhagavad Gita oder Das Hohe Lied enthaltend die Lehre der Unsterblichkeit,* translated into German by Franz Hartmann, second edition (Leipzig: Lotus-Verlag, 1904), 15f. This translation into English by Nicholas Goodrick-Clarke.

10. Friedemann Horn, *Und es war Abend und es war Morgen* (Zurich: Swedenborg Verlag, [n.d]), 15.

11. See the research of the clinical psychologist Wilson Van Dusen, *Der Mensch im Kraftfeld jenseitiger Welt* (Zurich: Swedenborg Verlag, 1979), esp. chap. 6. Van Dusen believes he has found a justification for Swedenborg's statement, inasmuch as human life is subject to a hierarchy of spirits. [In English, see Wilson Van Dusen, *The Presence of Other Worlds: The Psychological/Spiritual Findings of Emanuel Swedenborg* (1974; West Chester, Penna.: Chrysalis Books, 1991.]

12. Quoted in Gerhard Gollwitzer, *Die Geisterwelt ist nicht verscholssen* (Zurich: Swedenborg Verlag, 1966), 36.

13. John Klimo, *Channeling: Investigations on Receiving Information from Paranormal Sources* (Berkeley, Calif.: North Atlantic Books, 1998), 120.

14. Arthur Ford, *The Life beyond Death,* (London: W.H. Allen, 1972), 101.

15. Klimo, *Channeling*, 278–279. Klimo refers to Wilson van Dusen's *The Presence of Other Worlds* and quotes a passage from Swedenborg's preface to *Heaven and Hell*, which simply states: "Today's churchman knows almost nothing about heaven, hell or his own life after death. Moreover, Klimo considers all revelations as "channeling" without distinction, for example the Book of Revelation, Nostradamus, Swedenborg and Edgar Cayce (185).

Hans-Jürgen Ruppert emphasizes that Swedenborg was no spiritualist but still discusses him along with occultism, spiritualism, and channeling in his book *Okkultismus: Geisterwelt oder Neue Weltgeist?* (Wiesbaden: Coprint, 1990). Ruppert relies exclusively on foreign sources, for example, repeating Balzac's description of Swedenborg's vocational vision, Kant's remarks about Swedenborg, or Wilhelm Lütger's review of Swedenborg's influence on Kant and Goethe. There is also an extract from Jung-Stilling's *Theorie der Geisterkunde* (1807) concerning Swedenborg (202–221).

Authors John Ankerborg and John Welden describe Swedenborg as a "famous medium" in their highly critical discussion of modern channeling and spiritualism. In utter ignorance of the subject, they describe his work as devilish charlatanry; and in their tirade against spiritualism, they erroneously claim that Swedenborg founded his own "church," which has ever since ceaselessly spread spiritualistic revelations and which may be counted as the most antibiblical and anti-Christian tracts ever printed. John Ankerborg and John Welden, *Standpunkt: Channeling* (Asslar: Schulte & Gerth, 1989), 22f.

Colin Wilson relies exclusively on Wilson van Dusen, *The Presence of Other Worlds* when discussing Swedenborg. Colin Wilson, *Afterlife* (New York: Doubleday Dolphin, 1985), 16–24.

16. Quoted in Gerhard Gollewitzer, *Die durchsichtige Welt* (Zurich: Swedenborg Verlag, 1966), 19.

17. Immanuel Kant, *Träume eines Geistersehers, erläutert durch Träume der Metaphysik in Werke*, ed. Wilhelm Weischedel, 6 vols. (Darmstadt: Wissenschaftliche Buchgesellschaft, 1960), I, 973, 980. Concerning Kant's motive for ridiculing Swedenborg with his infamous criticism of *Arcana Coelestia*, see Ernst Benz, "*The Mysterious Datum: Zu Kants Kritik an Swedenborg*," in Ernst Benz, *Vision und Offenbarung: Gesammelte Swedenborg-Aufsätze* (Zurich: Swedenborg Verlag, 1979), 155–199. Because of Kant's interest in Swedenborg, his visions and extrasensory perceptions, Kant gradually fell under the suspicion of becoming an "apologist for spiritualism." Therefore, Kant delivered a counterblast to escape reproach (Benz, 157). Kant never denied the supersensual world but considered it unprovable. Swedenborg derives his unprovable knowledge from illumination, while Kant regards this kind of understanding as improbable. Thus, a direct comparison between Kant and Swedenborg is fundamentally impossible. See also Roland Begermat, "Swedenborg und Kant: ein andauernders Missverständnis, erklärt durch die Unvereinbarkeit der Standpunkte," in *Emanuel Swedenborg: Naturforscher und Kundiger der Überwelt* (Begleitbuch zu einer Ausstellung und Vortragsreihe in der Württembergischen Landesbibliothek Stuttgart), 74–76). However, Gottlieb Florschütz risks this comparison in his work *Swedenborg's verborgene Wirkung auf Kant* (Würzburg: Koenigshausen & Neumann, 1992). Chiefly

concerned with Swedenborg's ambivalent influence on Kant, he offers no insight into Swedenborg's own work. [In English, see Gottlieb Florschütz, *Swedenborg and Kant: Emanuel Swedenborg's Mystical View of Mankind and the Dual Nature of Humankind in Immanuel Kant,* trans. George F. Dole (West Chester, Penna.: Swedenborg Foundation, 1992).]

18. Florschütz, *Swedenborg's verborgene Wirkung auf Kant,* 97f.

19. Ernst Benz, *Vision und Offenbarung,* 121–153.

20. Friedemann Horn, *Schelling und Swedenborg: Ein Beitrag zur Problemgeschichte des deutschen Idealismus und zur Geschichte Swedenborgs in Deutschland* (Zurich: Swedenborg Verlag, 1954). [In English, Friedemann Horn, *Schelling and Swedenborg: Mysticism and German Idealism,* trans. George F. Dole (West Chester, Penna.: Swedenborg Foundation, 1997).]

21. C. G. Jung, *Memories, Dreams, Reflections,* ed. Aniela Jaffé, translated by Richard and Clara Winston (London: Fontana, 1983), 120.

22. See Helen Keller, *Light in My Darkness,* edited by Ray Silverman, 2nd edition (West Chester, Penna.: Chrysalis Books, 2000).

23. See Robin Larsen, ed., *Emanuel Swedenborg: A Continuing Vision* (New York: Swedenborg Foundation, 1988).

Chapter 2: The All-Embracing Whole

1. Quoted by Nick Herbert, *Quantum Reality: Beyond the New Physics* (London: Rider, 1985), 177.

2. Stephen Hawking, *A Brief History of Time: From the Big Bang to Black Holes* (London and New York: Bantam, 1988), 175.

3. Fritjof Capra, *The Tao of Physics: An Exploration of the Parallels between Modern Physics and Eastern Mysticism,* 3rd ed. (Boston: Shambhala Publications, 1991), 20.

4. Arthur Koestler, *Der Mensch—Irrläufer der Evolution* (Frankfurt am Main: Fischer Verlag, 1989), 28.

5. Capra, 131.

6. Ibid., 130.

7. Nick Herbert, *Quantum Reality,* 57; 69.

8. Albert Einstein and Leopold Infeld, *The Evolution of Physics* (New York: Simon and Schuster, 1938), 31.

9. Gary Zukav, *The Dancing Wu Li Masters: An Overview of the New Physics* (New York: Bantam, 1980), 107f.

10. Werner Heisenberg, *Physics and Beyond: Encounters and Conversations,* trans. Arnold J. Pomerans (London: George Allen and Unwin, 1971), 41. [original title: *Das Teil und Das Ganze*].

11. George Dole, "An Image of God in a Mirror," in *Emanuel Swedenborg: A Continuing Vision*, op. cit., 378).

12. Capra, op. cit., 51.

13. Capra finds the concept that every particle contains all the others not only in Eastern mysticism, but also in the "Western mystical thought, moreover in a strophe of the English visionary painter, engraver and poet, William Blake (1757–1827):

    To see a world in a grain of sand
    And a heaven in a wild flower,
    Hold infinity in the palm of your hand,
    And eternity in an hour."

    Capra, 297. Moreover, Swedenborg exercised a great influence on Blake for a time, who received his works during the 1780s in London. See Harvey F. Bellin, "Blake's 'Opposition is True Friendship': Swedenborg's influences on William Blake," in *Emanuel Swedenborg: A Continuing Vision*, 91–114.

14. Donald Factor, ed. *Unfolding Meaning: A Weekend of Dialogue with David Bohm*, (Mickleton, England): Foundation House, 1985), 10–11.

15. Ibid., 11.

16. Ibid., 31.

17. Ibid., 13.

18. Ibid., 52–55.

19. Quoted by Gerhard Gollwitzer, *Die durchsichtige Welt* (Zurich: Swedenborg Verlag, 1966), 68.

20. Quoted in Michael Talbot, "Swedenborg and the Holographic Paradigm," in *Emanuel Swedenborg, A Continuing Vision*, 446.

21. Gary Zukav, *The Dancing Wu Li Masters*, 194.

22. John Briggs and F. David Peat, *Turbulent Mirror: An Illustrated Guide to Chaos Theory and the Science of Wholeness,* second edition (New York: Harper & Row, 1990), 110–112.

23. Ibid., 62f.

24. Ibid., 110.

25. Factor, *Unfolding Meaning,* 150–152.

26. Ibid., 23.

27. Zukav, *Dancing Wu Li Masters*, 156.

28. Capra, *Tao of Physics*, 203.

29. Ibid., 69.

30. Zukav, 207.

31. Capra, 285.

32. Ibid., 80.

33. Zukav, 193.

34. Nick Herbert, *Quantum Reality*, 64, 40.

35. Capra, 69.

36. David Bohm quoted in Rupert Sheldrake, *The Presence of the Past: Morphic Resonance and the Habits of Nature* (London: Collins, 1988), 304.

37. Quoted in Nick Herbert, *Quantum Reality*, 112.

38. Einstein and Infeld, *Evolution of Physics*, 27.

39. Zukav, 285–290.

40. Quoted in Zukav, 294.

41. Herbert, 214.

42. Herbert, 242. A young physicist of the GSI Institut (Society for Heavy Ion Research) in Darmstadt tells me that Bell's Theorem does not appear in any physics textbook. It is not recognized in physics.

43. Capra, 318.

44. *Physik und Transcendenz: Die große Physiker unseres Jahrhundert über ihre Begegnung mit dem Wunderbaren*, ed. Hans-Peter Dürr (Berne: Scherz, 1966), 38, 107.

45. Burkhard Heim, *Der kosmische Erlebnisraum des Menschen* (Innsbruck: Resch Verlag, 1988) 21, 45.

46. Rupert Sheldrake, *A New Science of Life: The Hypothesis of Formative Causation* (London: Blond and Briggs, 1981), 206f.

47. Sheldrake, *Presence of the Past*, 324.

48. Factor, *Unfolding Meaning*, 172.

49. Quoted in Dürr, *Physics and Transcendence*, 160.

Chapter 3: Consciousness

1. Nick Herbert, *Quantum Reality*, op. cit., 249.

2. Stephano Sabetti, *Lebensenergie: Erscheinungsform und Wirkungsweise—ein ganzheitliches Modell* (Reinbek: Rowohlt, 1987).

3. Ibid., 81.

4. Robert Avens, "The Subtle Realm: Corbin, Sufism, and Swedenborg" in Larsen, *Emanuel Swedenborg: A Continuing Vision*, 382–391; Henry de Geymueller,

Swedenborg und die ubersinnliche Welt (Zurich: Swedenborg Verlag, 1963), 132–164.

5. Sabetti, *Lebensenergie,* 97f.

6. Factor, *Unfolding Meaning,* op. cit., 102.

7. Ibid., 103.

8. Sabetti, 92. Cf. Factor, 131–132.

9. Charles Leadbeater and Annie Besant, *Thought-Forms: A Record of Clairvoyant Investigation* (1901; rpt. Wheaton, Ill.: Theosophical Publishing House, 1969), 26–30.

10. Sheldrake, *A New Science of Life,* op. cit., 96.

11. Sheldrake, *The Presence of the Past,* 109.

12. Sheldrake, *A New Science of Life,* 196; Sheldrake, *The Presence of the Past,* 285.

13. Henry de Geymüller, *Swedenborg und die übersinnliche Welt* (Zurich: Swedenborg Verlag, 1963), 150.

14. Sheldrake, *The Presence of the Past,* 250–251.

15. Sheldrake, *A New Science of Life,* 113.

16. Ibid., 92f, 196.

17. Sheldrake, *The Presence of the Past,* 324.

18. Ibid., 268.

19. Ibid., 284.

20. Ibid., 303.

21. Ibid., 263–265.

22. Ibid., 322.

23. *The Upanishads,* translated and edited by Juan Mascaró (London and New York: Penguin, 1965), 139–140.

24. *Die Bhagavad Gita,* translated into German by Franz Hartmann (Leipzig: Lotus-Verlag, 1904), 124. Translation into English by Nicholas Goodrick-Clarke.

25. Inge von Wedemeyer, *Weltformel "Liebe": Ebenso aktuelle wie zeitlose Themen im Lichte der Meditation* (Leimen: Kristkeitz Verlag, 1990), 84.

Chapter 4: Spiritual Rebirth

1. Ernst Benz, *Emanuel Swedenborg: Scientist and Visionary,* translated by Nicholas Goodrick-Clarke (West Chester, Penna.: Swedenborg Foundation, forthcoming).

2.   Here "earth" signifies the outer, "heaven" the inner world of the spiritual man (*Arcana Coelestia* 89).

3.   Transpersonal psychology assumes that people can only find the truth in themselves, and only then can one speak of real "knowledge," which Charles Tart defines "as an immediately given experiential feeling of congruence between two different kinds of experience, a feeling of matching." Charles T. Tart, "Science, Sates of Consciousness, and Spiritual Experiences: The Need for State-Specific Sciences," in *Transpersonal Psychologies*, edited by Charles Tart (London: Routledge & Kegan Paul, 1975), 10–58 (the quotation appears on page 20).

4.   Von Wedemeyer, op. cit., 106.

5.   Sarvepalli Radhakrishnan, *Recovery of Faith* (New York: Harper & Brothers, 1955), 125.

6.   Henry Corbin, "Herméneutique spirituelle comparée: (I. Swedenborg – II. Gnose Ismaélienne)," *Eranos Jahrbuch* 33 (1964): 71–176 (101ff, 160).

7.   Inge von Wedemeyer, *Schicksal der Menschheit* (Calw: Schatzkammer Verlag, 1990), 178.

8.   Upanishads, 148f.

9.   Stephen Larsen, *Reise nach innen* (Zurich: Swedenborg Verlag, 1986), 28. Larsen gives an exhaustive report of Swedenborg's breathing technique in comparison with Indian yoga practices, 23–42.

10.   *Die Bhagavad Gita*, translated into German by Franz Hartmann (Leipzig: Lotus-Verlag, 1904), 47. This translation into English by Nicholas Goodrick-Clarke.

11.   Ibid., 102f.

12.   Ernst Benz, *Emanuel Swedenborg*; Stephen Larsen, *Reise nach innen*, 42–54.

13.   Cf. *Conjugial Love* 185, *True Christian Religion* 33, *Arcana Coelestia* 144.

14.   Felix Prochaska, *Heidnische Religionen und das Alte Wort* (Zurich: Swedenborg Verlag, 1974) attempts to substantiate Swedenborg's thesis that the Word is the fundamental meaning of many old religions.

15.   On the Word in Indian and Christian religions, see Joseph Leeming, *Yoga and the Bible: the Yoga of the Divine Word* (London: George Allen & Unwin, 1963), 38: "All life and energy in the universe come from the Divine Word. It is a power that is mightier than any known on earth, for it is the power behind all other powers."

16.   Quoted in Stephen Larsen, *Reise nach innen*, 55.

17.   Upanishads, 183.

18.   Stephen Larsen, *Reise nach innen*, 44.

Chapter 5: The New Age

1. Ernst Benz, *Vision und Offenbarung: Gesammelte Swedenborg-Aufsätze* (Zurich: Swedenborg Verlag, 1979), 29ff; and Ernst Benz, *Emanuel Swedenborg: Scientist and Visionary*, forthcoming.

2. Ernst Benz, *Emanuel Swedenborg*, forthcoming.

3. Ibid.

4. Ralph Waldo Emerson, *Representative Men: Seven Lectures* (London: Henry G. Bohn, 1850).

5. Rupert Sheldrake, *The Presence of the Past*, 308.

6. For an excellent explanation of the meaning of usefulness in Swedenborgian terms, see Wilson Van Dusen, "Uses: A Way of Personal and Spiritual Growth," in *The Country of Spirit: Selected Writings* (San Francisco: J. Appleseed & Co., 1992), 61–87.

7. Renate von Scholtz-Wiesner, *Lichtpfad der Menschheit: die Botschaft unserer Zeit* (Heilbronn: Heilbronn-Verlag, 1988), 147.

Chapter 6: Life after Death

1. Thorwald Dethlefsen, *Das Leben nach dem Leben: Gespräche mit Wiedergeborenen* (Munich: Goldmann, 1986), 120.

2. See, for example, Raymond A. Moody *Reflections on Life after Life* (Mockingbird Books: New York, 1977); *The Light Beyond* (Macmillan: London, 1988).

3. Peter Dinzelbacher, *An der Schwelle zum Jenseits: Sterbevisionen im interkulturellen Vergleich* (Freiburg: Herder Verlag, 1989).

4. Kurt Allgeier, *Niemand stirbt für ewig: Vorstellungen und Wandlungen der Reinkarnation. Tod, Metamorphose und Widergeburt* (Zurich: Diana Verlag, 1988), 173.

5. Rupert Sheldrake, *The Presence of the Past*, 221.

6. Ibid., pp. 221–222.

7. Carl Gustav Jung, *Memories, Dreams, Reflections*, recorded and edited by Aniela Jaffé, translated by Richard and Clara Winston (London: Fontana, 1983), 342–343.

8. Poul Lauritsen, *Reinkarnation und Freiheit* (Munich: Knaur Verlag, 1989), 39, 103.

9. Sri Aurobindo, *Der integrale Yoga* (Reinbek: Rowohlt Verlag, 1957), 45.

10. Inge von Wedemeyer, *Schicksal der Menschheit: Die Heimkehr des Sohnes, der verloren war* (Calw: Schatzkammer Verlag, 1990), 352.

11. Thomas Noack, "Leib und Auferstehungsleib" *Offene Tore* 4 (1989): 112.

12. Kurt Allgeier, 184.

13. Sri Aurobindo, 52.

BIBLIOGRAPHY OF WORKS BY
EMANUEL SWEDENBORG

Apocalypse Explained. 6 vols. Translated by John Whitehead. 2nd ed. West Chester, Penna: The Swedenborg Foundation, 1994–1998.

Apocalypse Revealed. 2 vols. Translated by John Whitehead. 2nd ed. West Chester, Penna: The Swedenborg Foundation, 1997.

Arcana Coelestia. 12 vols. Translated by John Clowes. Rvd. John F. Potts. 2nd ed.West Chester, Penna: The Swedenborg Foundation, 1995–1998. The first volume of this work is also available under the title *Heavenly Secrets.*

Charity: The Practice of Neighborliness. Translated by William F. Wunsch. Ed. William R. Woofenden. West Chester, Penna: The Swedenborg Foundation, 1995.

Conjugial Love. Translated by Samuel S. Warren. Rvd. Louis Tafel. 2nd ed. West Chester, Penna: The Swedenborg Foundation, 1998. This volume is also available under the title *Love in Marriage,* translated by David Gladish (West Chester, Penna.: Swedenborg Foundation, 1992).

Divine Love and Wisdom. Translated by John C. Ager. 2nd ed. West Chester, Penna: The Swedenborg Foundation, 1995. This volume is also available in a translation by George F. Dole.

Divine Providence. Translated by William Wunsch. 2nd ed. West Chester, Penna: The Swedenborg Foundation, 1996.

Four Doctrines. Translated by John F. Potts. 2nd ed. West Chester, Penna: The Swedenborg Foundation, 1997.

Heaven and Hell. Translated by John C. Ager. 2nd ed. West Chester, Penna: The Swedenborg Foundation, 1995. This volume is also available in a new translation by George F. Dole, New Century Edition of the Works of Emanuel Swedenborg (West Chester, Penna: The Swedenborg Foundation, 2000.).

The Heavenly City. Translated by Lee Woofenden. West Chester, Penna: The Swedenborg Foundation, 1993. Also known as *The New Jerusalem and Its Heavenly Doctrine* (see *Miscellaneous Theological Works,* below).

Journal of Dreams. Translated by J. J. G. Wilkinson. Introduction by Wilson Van Dusen. New York: The Swedenborg Foundation,1986. This work has also been issued in a new translation: Lars Bergquist, ed. *Swedenborg's Dream Diary.* Trans. Anders Hallengren. West Chester, Penna.: The Swedenborg Foundation, 2000.

119

The Last Judgment in Retrospect. Translated by and edited by George F. Dole. West Chester, Penna: The Swedenborg Foundation, 1996. This work is also know as *The Last Judgment and Babylon Destroyed* (see *Miscellaneous Theological Works,* below).

Miscellaneous Theological Works. Translated by John Whitehead. 2nd ed. West Chester, Penna: The Swedenborg Foundation, 1996. This volume includes *The New Jerusalem and Its Heavenly Doctrine, Earths in the Universe,* and *The Last Judgment and Babylon Destroyed,* among others.

Posthumous Theological Works. 2 vols. Translated by John Whitehead. 2nd ed. West Chester, Penna: The Swedenborg Foundation, 1996. These volumes include the autobiographical and theological extracts from Swedenborg's letters, additions to *True Christian Religion, The Doctrine of Charity, The Precepts of the Decalogue,* and collected minor works, among others.

True Christian Religion. 2 vols. Translated by John C. Ager. West Chester, Penna: The Swedenborg Foundation, 1996.

Worship and Love of God. Translated by Alfred H. Stroh and Frank Sewall. 2nd ed. West Chester, Penna: The Swedenborg Foundation, 1996.

INDEX

on thought, 50
Sophi, 76
soul
  after death, 97
  cosmos linked with, 33
  as essential element, 67
spiritual inertia, 69
spiritual influx, x–xi
spiritual rebirth
  beginning, 109
  chakras and, 60
  history of, 84
  knowledge through, 107
  later stages, 71
  peace through, 72–73
  preface to, 65, 66, 68, 69
  process, 58
  purpose, 79
  redemption through, 105
  struggle during, 70
  Swedenborg's, 75
  terrestrial, 101
spiritualistic practices, 9–10, 112n15
  popularity of, 103
  Swedenborg on, 8–9
Stapp, Henry Pierce, 32
Stevenson, Ian, xiii–xiv
Structure of Scientific Revolution (Kuhn), ix
success, 43, 44
Suzuki, Daisetz Teitaro, vii, 77
Swedenborg, Emanuel
  twentieth-century writers and, xi
  at Swedish Board of Mines, 3
  books to universities, 82
  breathing techniques, 7, 73–74
  discoveries anticipated by, 3
  early life, 1–2
  Eastern admirers, 77
  influence of, 10–13
  as Lutheran, 85
  psychological studies by, 4
  religious questions, 8
  research journeys, 2–3
  on spiritualist practices, 8–9
  supreme principle, 26
  transition to visionary, 4–6
  visions of, 5–8, 10
  writings as occult, 59

T
The Tao of Physics (Capra), 16
Tart, Charles, 117n3
tendencies, human, 44–45

thoughts
  origin, 50
  positive, 42–43
  realization of, 43
  spiritual, 41, 61
transpersonal psychology, 117n3

U
Ulrika, Louisa (Queen of Sweden), 9
uncertainty principle, 20
unity principle, 17–18
universe
  actualized, 87–88
  foundation, 23–25
  polarity, 27–28, 30
unity, 17–18
Upanishads, 54–55, 66, 73, 78, 89
usefulness, 89–90
utility, 89–90

V
Van Dusen, Wilson, 111n11
Varieties of Religious Experience (James), viii
visions
  high consciousness, 7
  Swedenborg's, 5–8, 10
visualization, 42
Von Høpken, Count Anders Johan, 10
Von Wedemeyer, Inge, 58, 103

W
wealth, 90
Welden, John, 112n15
wholeness, vii–viii
  holograms and, 21–23
will
  as essential element, 67
  outer, 71
  and spiritual rebirth, 70
wisdom
  genuine, 65, 67
  love and, 39–40, 41
Word of God
  Bible as, 76
  in various religions, 117n14, 117n15
work, 92

Y
yoga, 73–74

Z
Zukav, Gary, 19, 30